Enakshi Ganguly has been involved in research, advocacy and training on a wide range of human rights issues, such as displacement due to development, child rights, women rights and those concerning other marginalized groups since 1985. She is an Advisor at HAQ: Centre for Child Rights, which she founded in 1998 and co-directed till 2018. She has authored a number of publications, including reports, articles and edited volumes on a range of subjects related to forced displacement, land and housing rights, women and children. She is the co-convenor of the Working Group on Human Rights (WGHR) and is on the board of several organizations including the Child Rights International Network (CRIN, London) and, till recently, was also on the board of the Gender Centre of the Lal Bahadur Shastri National Academy of Administration (LBSNAA). She is an honorary professor at the National Law University, Odisha, and is currently Executive Director of the Housing and Land Rights Network, India. Enakshi was awarded the Ashoka Fellowship in 2003 and the REX Karmaveer Chakra award instituted by iCONGO in partnership with the United Nations.

Dr Kalpana Purushothaman is a member of the Juvenile Justice Board, Bangalore (Urban) and Adjunct Professor, Indian Institute of Psychology and Research (IIPR). She was formerly Senior Professional Counsellor and Senior Researcher, Juvenile Justice Program at the Centre for Child & the Law, National Law School of India University, Bangalore and has authored a book on child psychology for the judiciary. Dr Purushothaman was instrumental in establishing the first-of-its-kind corporate-government-judiciary and civil society partnership to set up the MAANASA Wellness Centre at the Observation Home, Bangalore, which provides a range of medical and mental health care services for children (and families) in conflict with the law. In 2022, she was nominated for the Children's Champion Award by the Delhi Commission for the Protection of Child Rights. She was awarded the Guru Shrestha Award, Karnataka in 2019 for her exemplary role as an exceptional and inspiring teacher for young people from different socio-economic backgrounds. Dr Purushothaman also works with survivors of violence and sexual abuse across all genders and is a trained, queer-affirmative therapist.

Puneeta Roy is a media professional who has worked in film and television for over three decades. Her interest in expressive arts has led her to conduct workshops with young people using theatre and the arts as tools for self-exploration and transformation. She has been deeply involved in working with Children in Conflict with Law at various government remand homes in North Delhi. In 2014, she founded The Yuva Ekta Foundation, through which she has expanded her work among underprivileged youth, working on issues of self-worth and self-esteem to empower young people heal their past and make more constructive choices in their lives. The Foundation has recently completed and released a two-year research study, *Building Emotional Intelligence and Self Esteem with Children in Conflict with Law using Expressive Arts and Psychodrama Therapy*, which yielded valuable data on the impact of reformative practices with young offenders in India.

JUVENILE, NOT DELINQUENT

Children in Conflict With the Law

ENAKSHI GANGULY

with **KALPANA PURUSHOTHAMAN**
and **PUNEETA ROY**

SPEAKING TIGER BOOKS LLP
125A, Ground Floor, Shahpur Jat, near Asiad Village,
New Delhi 110049

First published by Speaking Tiger Books 2023

ISBN: 978-93-5447-445-3
eISBN: 978-93-5447-458-3

10 9 8 7 6 5 4 3 2 1

Typeset in Minion Pro by SÜRYA, New Delhi
Printed at Chaman Enterprises, New Delhi

The hood made me realize that crime succeeds because crime
does one thing government doesn't do. Crime cares. Crime
is grassroots. Crime looks for young kids who need support
and a lifting hand. Crime offers internship programmes and
summer jobs and opportunities for advancement. Crime gets
involved in the community. Crime does not discriminate.

—Trevor Noah, Born a Crime

CONTENTS

FOREWORD

A guru of unpopular causes, a carer of children least cared about, a fearless truth-teller—the author of this book is known not only in India but around the world in the circles of those who work with and for children. She is known for her resolute advocacy, her unflinching criticism of injustice and her optimism that things can change.

Enakshi Ganguly has met kindred souls in many parts of the world, so she knows she is not alone. In India, and even in the writing of this book, she is not alone. As she explains, Puneeta Roy and the Yuva Ekta Team and Kalpana Purushothaman, who have contributed to the second part of this book, are individuals who share her obsession, her striving to call out injustice, and to put things right. India's children are fortunate to have these tigers fighting for them.

I remember when, back in 2014, India reported to the United Nations Committee on the Rights of the Child, Enakshi had travelled to Geneva to present an alternative report. Children in the criminal justice system were high on the agenda—by this time the Delhi gang rape case, which is an important point of departure in this book, had already happened. Pushback against India's specialized juvenile justice system was intense, and so was it, in India, against what was thought to be a system too lenient with criminal youth that deserved much worse. The Committee expressed serious concern about some aspects of India's juvenile justice system, and urged India to bring it fully in line with the Convention on the Rights of the Child. In that volatile atmosphere, Enakshi and her colleagues fought the unpopular fight in order to implement those recommendations back in India, preparing for and sitting in on court cases, speaking to a belligerent media, writing articles and persuading the legislature—trying to be the voice of reason.

The publication of this book marks an important anniversary in Enakshi's life as well. It was the year 1996. News came of the brutal flogging a boy in a Children's Home in India. The lack of outrage over this appalling incident had confronted Enakshi, as it did many others, with the distressing reality of children in conflict with the law and a desperate need for concrete action. Thus was HAQ born in 1998. And now, twenty-five years later, she has found a slice of time to share not only a personal account of her engagement with the system, but a succinct introduction to the birth and development of juvenile justice in India, and its pitfalls and achievements.

The themes of countering injustice are met in equal measure in this book with narratives of hope. Hope for children's reform, hope for better systems, more thoughtful law making, and more caring professionals. As Enakshi says, echoing the sentiments of all of us who work with or within the system: 'It's only hope that keeps us going.'

ANN SKELTON

Professor of Law at the Universities of Pretoria and Leiden, and Member of the UN Committee on the Rights of the Child

PROLOGUE

We were at a book reading by Paro Anand at Café Turtle. She was reading from her book on adolescents. Somehow the conversation veered towards how children these days 'mature faster'. And as has almost become a pattern over the last few years, the conversation moved to children and offending and of course the 'juvenile in the Nirbhaya case' and how he was the 'worst offender'.

I had come to the reading planning only to listen, to simply be part of an evening devoted to literature. But as the discussion about 'the juvenile' became more and more detailed, with loud repetitions of all the misinformation the media had spread, I could not resist speaking up. I put up my hand and said that the police officer investigating the case had actually clarified that although 'the juvenile' was present in the bus, the scene of the horrendous crime, he was not the most brutal as he had been depicted and that, in fact, the police had withdrawn this observation. The Juvenile Justice Board that was investigating the matter had said the same thing. Sadly, while the news about him being 'the brutal monster' had been flashed across the front pages of every newspaper, this news item was tucked away in the back pages, and hence remained un-read by most.

Suddenly, many heads turned to me. Some out of

curiosity and others to contradict. The fact that I have read the chargesheet and nowhere did I find the 'facts' the media had presented reflected in it enabled me to stand my ground.

At the end of the programme, Renuka Chatterjee of Speaking Tiger came and introduced herself to me. That is how this book was born.

India is not the only country in the world that treats 'juvenile delinquents' with suspicion and hatred. The fact that countries across the world have vacillated between extreme punitive to child sensitive and back to punitive laws over the years is proof of that. Who are these children, the young people who enter the 'system'? Do they ever 'reform'? Can they be placed back in society? These are questions that societies across the world have contended with periodically. This book is an effort to answer these questions.

I have been a human rights activist for the last four decades. In 1997, when I had first conceived of the idea of HAQ: Centre for Child Rights, it was in response to an incident of a child being hung from a fan and beaten to death in a Children's Home in Delhi a year previously. I was appalled at the lack of noise and protest around this incident, even by groups that said they were working on children's issues. The following year, I co-founded HAQ, named after the Urdu word for right. While most of my own experiences shared in the book are from my time as co-director of HAQ, a position I held till 2018, they're not confined only to that period.

An account of children in conflict with the law must necessarily be simultaneously an account of those adults who helped them navigate the system, people who never gave up on them. While I've dedicated a chapter in Part I to just such people that I've had the privilege of knowing or working with, a need was felt for first-person accounts that offer a glimpse of the lives of the children who offend and the work the former do among them.

Part 2 of this book thus includes testimonies by two women who chose to engage in this work. Both Puneeta Roy, and the Yuva Ekta Team, and Kalpana Purushothaman, who has been a member of a Juvenile Justice Board in Karnataka, did not start out as social workers or experts in juvenile justice. They simply meandered into working with young offenders and stayed on. In the process of helping these children heal and offering them the fresh start they needed, they found themselves healing and growing too. Their experiences show us the challenges of working with these children. But they also represent the hope that every child care worker is driven by.

We sincerely hope that this book, in its own small way, is able to change a few minds, to make them see these child offenders as victims rather than inveterate lawbreakers, and to make them realize that the way forward is through compassion, not retribution.

PART ONE

Introduction

YOURS, MINE AND OURS

We were out on a holiday. Our then teenage son had chosen to stay back in Delhi. Suddenly, the phone rang. It was our neighbour, who informed us the police had come to 'pick up' our son as another neighbour had lodged a complaint against him. We then spoke to our tearful son, who was completely clueless as to why the police had come and what he was supposed to have done. He sounded devastated and afraid. Apparently, our neighbours, a doctor couple, Mr and Mrs D's car had been vandalized and the windscreen broken. Dr (Mrs) D had examined the footage of the CCTV camera outside her home and saw two young boys, one of whom she insisted looked like our son, break her car's windscreen with a hockey stick.

Another kind neighbour had 'managed' to convince the police to wait till we returned. We rushed back to Delhi. We went to the house of Mr and Mrs D to look at the video footage. It contained grainy images of two young people passing by her car. There was no footage of anyone breaking her windscreen. She insisted that one of the boys carried a hockey stick and that it was our son. The faces were unclear— so it could be any boy. We left, asking her to file a complaint so that we could address the matter in court.

The police arrived again. All the neighbours watched what went on. Of course, the man in charge was not a Child Welfare Police Officer[1]—a specially designated police person who can handle a case of a child alleged to have offended as per the juvenile justice law. In fact, he was most offended on being asked if he was. He tried to intimidate us, and even to explore if he could extract some money. Since we insisted on paperwork and proof, he gave up and left. There was no complaint and no court case. But for the first time, we as a family experienced what it must be like for those parents and their children whom the police come to apprehend—rightly or wrongly—and the uncertainty and humiliation that is part of it.

When I was younger, I remember the adults always telling us, 'Only the wearer knows where the shoe pinches.' Albeit a bit archaic in its syntax, that still holds true. Although I had worked with children in conflict with the law for many years, for the first time we as a family realized where the shoe pinches! And it really hurt—watching our son being dragged through the mud and feeling humiliated. The only thing that helped him from being scarred for life was that we, his parents, believed in him and were there to support him. It also helped that the rest of the neighbours who had known him since his childhood had supported him when his parents were not there.

A few years ago, I found myself before the Supreme Court of India in a joint petition filed by my friend and comrade Shantha Sinha and myself, pleading that the apex court enquire into the reported illegal detention of children and ensure that their rights were protected following the abrogation of Article 370 of the Constitution of India, which had granted special status to Jammu and Kashmir. All or most of these children had been picked up for 'preventive detention'.

On 13 December 2019, the last day of hearing in the Supreme Court, I sat at the back of the courtroom, all by myself. A report had been submitted by the Jammu and Kashmir High Court Juvenile Justice Committee to the Supreme Court based on our prayers. As per the report, all detentions were in accordance with law. The bench, comprising of Justices N.V. Ramana, Subhash Reddy and B.R. Gavai, said that it had examined the report and found it to be satisfactory; they were convinced that no child was detained illegally.[2] When our lawyer, Huzefa Ahmadi contested the legality of the detentions, pointing out that as per all the records submitted to the courts, seventy-nine children were detained under Section 107 of the Code of Criminal Procedure (CrPC), and that preventive detention of minors was illegal, Justice Gavai interjected, 'But they were released the same day. Have you seen these children? Are you aware what 15-year-olds are capable of doing these days?' Justice Reddy asked if it could be termed detention if many were released after only a few hours. 'It has happened in Hyderabad too where people are restrained for a while and released. Can we call it detention?' he remarked.[3]

When Huzefa Ahmadi asked for a copy of the report, I heard the judges say something to the effect that since we keep challenging the reports we receive, we would be given a copy of the report but the court would not entertain any challenge against the findings! I thought I may have heard wrongly, but this was also reported later in the media.

As I watched from the other end of the courtroom, I remember thinking to myself: Indeed, who are *these* children? What are they capable of? Did they look any different from the children we see every day? And really, why did we care so much? Enough to have ourselves vilified in open court by none other than the Solicitor General of India, Mr Tushar Mehta, who asked loudly: 'Does a lady sitting in Delhi decide what is happening in J&K?' I recall hearing him refer to me as the 'woman/lady from Delhi' several times—and not to pay a compliment! Earlier he had said that our intentions were malicious and we were only seeking publicity.

The fact is that Shantha and I were deeply concerned. We could barely sleep at night as news reports of young children being detained—the youngest being eight years old—kept pouring in. We felt that the Supreme Court of India would be equally moved by the situation of these children. That is why we had filed a petition. Were we wrong in having this hope of our highest court?

The last time I had sat in Court No. 1 of the Supreme Court was in 2013, when Dr Subramanian Swamy had filed a case challenging the constitutionality of the Juvenile Justice Act (JJ Act), after the rape and murder of the young woman named Jyoti Singh, which came to be known as the Nirbhaya case. The court was also hearing petitions filed by the deceased's parents and others, all of them challenging the juvenile justice law and seeking harsher punishment for the underage offender. Some organizations, including HAQ, which I was a part of, had filed an intervention challenging this. We had also arranged for a lawyer to represent the juvenile offender, since he had been made a party to the case filed by Dr Swamy.[4]

Watching the young woman's parents sitting across the aisle in court broke my heart. It's not as if I did not understand their loss or pain. No one in the world deserves to lose their child and suffer as they had. And yet, there we were, seen to be in an adversarial role because we were trying to protect the law on juvenile justice. To them, we were trying to save the young boy from being punished, thus obstructing justice for their daughter.

But that really was not the case. Who in their right mind would not want justice for the victim? We did want justice for their daughter, which included legal action against the young person involved in the case. But we also believe, as we did then, that children who offend must be dealt with under a special law meant for them. Unfortunately, it was clear that sharp dividing lines had been drawn.

This was not the first time I had found myself in this awkward situation with respect to this case and the ensuing debate on the juvenile justice law itself. The media revelled in turning ours into an adversarial position. I recall I was called by a television channel for a telephonic interview to discuss the proposed amendments to the Juvenile Justice Act, 2000. I also recall specifically saying that while I was happy to discuss the law, I would not wish to be on the programme if 'Nirbhaya's' parents were to also be on it. I did not want to be contesting their demand for change in the law which came from a position of extreme pain over a personal loss. I was assured that they would not be there. As I got on air, I realized that I had been lied to. The channel had turned it into a them-versus-us drama, the sufferers versus those who did not seem to care for victims, the child rights activist versus the women's rights activist. A lot of versus!

But that was not how it was meant to be. What we were advocating for was protecting the rights of children *and* the rights of women; protecting the rights of children who offend even as they are held accountable *and* the rights of victims. Sadly, the narrative around juvenile justice—the law, the children who come in conflict with the law, how they should be treated—had been appropriated by politics and vested interests. There were thousands of children across the country who were caught in the 'system', but no one had paid any attention to them. It took one horrifying and gruesome incident for the 'conscience of the nation' to awaken. Till then the nation did not want to know, nor did it care.

My initial engagement with juvenile justice goes back to 1993, when I was the deputy director of the Multiple Action Research Group (MARG)—a non-profit organization that provides socio-legal services to the poor and marginalized. In fact, I stumbled into it. I knew nothing about the juvenile justice law or the institutions that children are placed in using the law. Some friends were visiting us. One of them was the wife of a mountaineer/trekker friend of my husband. She suddenly said that a doctor friend of hers had made a shocking discovery in one of her visits to an institution on the outskirts of Delhi. It was part of her medical college's outreach programme. She had found out that a small boy had died in that home. He died because the caretaker sat on his chest and choked him; he was angry because the child would soil his bed. This doctor couldn't figure out what to do about it.

'Why doesn't your friend report this?' I asked naively.

'Oh! You know how it is…she doesn't want to—she wants to remain anonymous.'

I was young too, and not very 'old' in the 'sector' either. I was outraged. I just couldn't understand why this doctor would not wish to report what appeared to be a case of murder of a young boy by someone who was supposed to be protecting him. It was only many years later that I realized that people do not like to 'report' violence—not in their own homes or around them. That they don't want to get involved with police and courts—'*Court kachehri mein nahi parna*' is the common refrain. There is always a deathly silence that surrounds violence.

So on that day I asked our friend, 'So why are you telling me this?'

'Oh, you are with an NGO, so I thought you may know what to do,' she replied.

Did I? I was not sure. In fact, I did *not* know what to do.

But the story stayed with me. MARG, which I was working with, was founded by Dr Vasudha Dhagamwar (1940–2014), who in my opinion was one of the best minds on law and philosophy that India has ever had. I spoke to Vasudha. She was horrified and incensed. 'Do you think we can do something?' I asked. 'Do you think we should visit this institution?' Vasudha, who had, years earlier, in 1980, while conducting research work in Bihar, serendipitously discovered four young Pahadiya tribal boys in a jail as undertrials[5] and had taken their case to the Supreme Court, agreed that we should.

But at MARG, we had not worked on juvenile justice issues. The new law had just come into existence in 1986. So for me it was all very new. Reading the law, we found a provision for visitors to visit these institutions. But how did one get listed as a visitor? The law did not specify that.

My colleague in MARG, Aasha Ramesh was more resourceful. She found a way to approach the Delhi Government, walk into the office of the Director, Women and Child Development, show him the provision in the law and make a request. And voila! We had the permission. The only condition was, we were not to speak to the press. He also said that we were to send him regular reports. We agreed.

That's it. We were set to go. But this 'home' felt so far away. The first day we tried to reach the Children's Home by bus. We took a very long time to get there. After changing two buses, when we reached the Children's Home, we barely had any time to convince the superintendent that we hadn't come to spy on or report him. Well, actually, we had. But we were not telling him that. All we said was that we had been given permission to enter as 'visitors' by the government, as per the law. We would come twice a month to interact with the inmates.

That was my first entry into an 'institution'. Till then I had only visited an orphanage run by Mother Teresa's Sisters of Charity, in Kolkata, where I had seen rows of babies in cradle-swings. They were so adorable that I had wanted to pick them up and hug them. The boys in this home were very different. They were unkempt, rude, aggressive and even abusive. They were filthy and smelly. The older ones eyed us suspiciously. The caretakers and teachers warned us about them. I will have to admit, I was a tiny bit apprehensive myself. The locks on the gates (yes, there were two of them) opened to let us in and then closed shut. In those early days, we would look back fearfully as the heavy gates shut behind us. Those were not days of cell phones, so really no one could reach us.

But we kept going to the Home as bona fide 'visitors'. All we did was chat with the boys, the staff—and occasionally plan an activity, which the boys sometimes very reluctantly participated in.

The boys were not allowed into the grounds to play for fear they may scale the walls and escape. Children escaping meant a memo or even suspension of the staff. They could not risk that. Cooped up inside the walls, adolescent energy turned into 'combustible' energy resulting in fights and brawls. We needed to change that.

Everyone was hostile—the staff, who were suspicious of being found out, and the older boys, who did not like being 'disturbed'. The only ones we could interact with were the little ones and that's where we started.

As our visits became regular, and we became familiar faces, tentative hands of friendship began to be extended. We could walk through the corridors, visit the kitchen or the dormitories without being trailed. As the hostility from the staff eased somewhat and they got used to our visits, small and big changes began to be seen—at least in the physical space. Toilets started to smell less, the kitchen began to look cleaner and more hygienic, the dormitories were less untidy and filthy. These were changes our mere presence as outsiders brought about. They suddenly felt the need to put their best foot forward.

Slowly, based on conversations with the superintendent and his team, it was agreed that the younger children, who found themselves locked in at all times, would go to the neighbourhood government school. Fear that they would escape was the reason they had not been allowed until then. It meant caretakers would have to accompany them to and from, and they had not wanted to take that responsibility. But now, as they began to do so, no boy attempted to escape.

The children were even allowed to come with us in batches to the ground to play. That was the biggest win of all—watching the glee on their faces when they finally had the freedom of being able to touch the grass and smell the air. Later, one of the caretakers even took the initiative to start a kitchen garden with some of the boys.

The lady doctor who would dispense only ibuprofen tablets for everything—be it fever, skin infection or stomach ache—was replaced. She refused to touch the boys and so never got to see that most of them had scabies, that head lice was endemic and some even had body lice. Before coming to the children's institution, she had been a family planning doctor, which back then basically comprised of dispensing contraceptives. She felt no empathy for the boys. If anything, she was irritated by them. Although she may have secretly been relieved about being posted out, she nonetheless called the MARG office and spoke to the administrator. She asked if I worked there and threatened dire consequences. That was the first time I was confronted with the fact that this work was not without its pitfalls. After her, several other staff members too were transferred and replaced.

Since we were ourselves so unfamiliar with mental health issues, we couldn't identify any symptoms. Looking back now, I am sure there must have been many who were suffering from them. There was addiction too, and the staff, both male and female, were the suppliers. The older boys even had sex with some of the female staff who supplied the *bidis*. Our unexposed eyes would have cause to pop out and our eyebrows rise high every day. But we would pretend not be shocked.

It was during these visits that I met OP, who was around 15 or 16 years old. He was one of the 'older' boys. But he stood out by his quiet and serious demeanour. He was one of the first of the 'older' boys who slowly warmed up to us and began to speak to us. He helped us break the ice and gradually build a rapport with the older boys. He was one of the few allowed to leave the 'home' and attend the neighbourhood school. Even the most aggressive bullies did not trouble him. They let him be, and even showed him quiet respect for his scholarly attributes.

Fed up with her life, OP told us, his mother had taken him and his brother by the hand and dragged them to the well to jump in. Petrified, 10-year-old OP pulled himself free of his mother's grip and ran. He did not stop running till he reached a railway station and jumped onto a train. He did not know where the train was headed, and when he got off, he found himself in Chandigarh. He did not know where Chandigarh was, but read the name on the board. Hungry and tired he scrounged for food and begged on trains. One day he found himself on a moving train that brought him to Delhi. The police found him wandering on the railway platform and brought him to the Observation Home (Reception Centre) in Feroz Shah Kotla. This was before the enactment of the Juvenile Justice (Care and Protection of Children) Act, 2000. As per the 1986 version of the Juvenile Justice Act, police brought all children to a central place—like the Observation Home in Feroz Shah Kotla—from where they were divided into two groups: the *neglected* children and the *delinquent* children. OP was declared to be neglected and sent to a Juvenile Home (now called Children's Home), where children who had been abandoned, orphaned, abused, trafficked, etc.—or in 'need of care and protection' as they are now called—were housed.

He remembers how scared he was. He also said he was so hungry that he was contemplating stealing when the police found him. Had he stolen, he would not have been in the Children's Home. Instead, he would have been taken to a Special Home and referred to as a juvenile delinquent.

OP was able to finish school and then he joined an ITI

(an industrial training institute that offers vocational and technical training) for a diploma course. He moved on with his life and even went back home and made peace with his family. He once came home with a sari for me that he had bought with his earnings. I never saw him after that. But that sari remains my most treasured gift, one that I shall pass on to my daughter as an heirloom.

It was in this Juvenile Home that I recognized, for the first time, how thin the line dividing the two categories of children is—children who are in need of care and protection (CNCP) and those who are in conflict with the law (CICL).[6] A desperate child can become an offender. If caught, his or her life changes completely. If he is not caught, apprehended or arrested, he is a child who needs love, care and attention—even the law deems that. That is why the juvenile justice system addresses both categories of children. This book, however, is about those who 'offend' and are therefore in conflict with the law.

Everyone who speaks of '*delinquent* children' is actually asking, even when they're not, in the most outraged voice—'Do you know what they are like? *Those* children?' In 2019, the honourable judges of the Kashmir Bench of the Supreme Court had reminded me of this very fact when they asked in open court: 'Have you seen these children? Are you aware what 15-year-olds are capable of doing these days?' Once again, I realized how any child could be declared a delinquent. And once declared so, their life changes for ever.

That is why I like to do an exercise in my training sessions with the police, judicial officers, staff of the juvenile justice system and NGO workers.[7] I ask the participants to close their eyes, imagine a child offender and then describe him or her. The descriptions range from huge bodies, bloodshot eyes to even a funky hairdo. It's amazing how many even say dark (referring to their complexion). There are some who add that 'they' are from the slums and *bastis*. Most do not imagine girls.

'But almost every third boy on the street today, cutting across class, has a funky hairdo. Many young people live in slums and *bastis*…are they all potential criminals?' I ask. 'No,' says the group. 'And dark? Does the colour of the skin define character?' I press on. Most often there is silence. Clearly, prejudices run deep and we still discriminate by colour and where people live. So I push further. 'Dark skin. Or based on where they live. Don't you think that we are being discriminatory?' There is silence again.

I further the discussion. 'Does the child who is alleged to have killed a little boy in the public school in Gurugram[8] fit that description? Does that little 4-year-old boy who put a pencil in the vagina of his classmate[9] fit that description? Does the boy who ran a man over in his father's Mercedes[10] fit that description?' I ask. 'And what about those boys from a public school who took their classmate for a "date" and murdered her?'[11]

Pat comes the response, 'But the juvenile in the 16 December case was described in the media as the worst perpetrator.' 'He was from the streets and we hear he is Muslim.'

'But have any of you seen him? How do you know he fits this description?' I ask. And once again, I am met with silence.

What becomes clear after such repeated conversations is that there is an image of a *child offender*—a *juvenile delinquent*—in people's minds. And this description is not based on any real interaction. It's based completely on prejudice and othering. Even when pointed in a different direction, the tendency is to turn right back to the prejudicial assumptions. That is the comfort zone.

The vocal middle-class demand for a harsh law for child offenders, one that says child offenders must be punished just like adults, is therefore not surprising. It is a demand driven by prejudice; it is a law for 'them'—'those children out there'—children who fit into a certain prototype, not least of which are the characteristics of being poor, unwashed and unkempt. Of course caste and religion are also thrown into the pot. The bottom line is, they are not like *us*. And they cannot be *our* children.

Working among the CICL, we are often forced to ask ourselves why it is that we see children from only a certain socio-economic category enter the system. Can it be that 'middle class' and rich children do not offend—ever? If they do, then do they not need to 'reform'? So why do they bypass the system and how?

In the time I've spent working on juvenile justice I have come across only very few cases in which a child from a 'privileged class' has been brought into the juvenile justice system. Two of these I've mentioned above: the case of the boy who ran over a man while driving his father's Mercedes; and that of the boy who is accused of murdering a small child in a public school in Gurugram. And I dare say this happened because there was a sudden rise in consciousness about juvenile delinquency following the Nirbhaya case. But even when they do enter the system, power and privilege are used to ensure that such children leave it just as fast. A random visit to a juvenile facility, and who we find in them, is enough to bear out this reality.

It is assumed that the middle-class or the rich kid never offends. Which is simply not true as the examples above amply show. Besides, we've all heard enough anecdotes from our own friends and family to know that that cannot be the case.

On 9 June 2022, the morning headlines were about a young boy in Lucknow who had killed his mother because she wouldn't let him play online games like PUBG.[12] This boy allegedly shot his mother using the licensed pistol of his father, who is in the Army, and hid her body inside their house in Lucknow for three days using a room freshener to mask the smell. He even frightened his younger sister into silence.

As I read this news, I recalled another incident from about two decades ago, in which an adolescent boy had beaten his mother to death with a hammer in an upper-class neighbourhood in Delhi. In fact, friends who lived in the same colony often remind me of this case. After that no one heard of him or the case. It was not the age of social media and an irate public did not step out onto the streets. Delhi is a 'village', as one discovers after living in it for many years. Gossip mills rule the roost. Several years later, the grapevine reported that his father had 'worked the system' and sent him abroad to study. So there were no TV debates about his 'horrendous act', the family and every other gory detail. The nation, it seems, did not want to know. At the same time, I cannot but wonder if his father sent him for counselling to deal with the trauma he must have had to deal with himself—which is inevitable. How is he coping with the trauma? Did it in any way affect him psychologically? What about the family? How did they cope?

This phenomenon of privilege is not confined to India

alone. In the USA, for example, African American, Latino, and Native American children receive much harsher treatment than European American children—the white children. The differential perception and treatment of African American children has deep historical roots in the United States. And, further, it has been observed that when children in the juvenile justice system are thus viewed as children of the 'other', the justice system becomes an instrument of repression and control instead of justice. It in turn feeds into existing racial disparities and perpetuates them 'legally'.[13] In India it can take different, though essentially similar, forms—injustice based on class, caste, religion and ethnicity.

What kind of long-term impact does the experience of having been an 'offender' leave on the minds of children? Do they ever forget it? If not, what is the kind of support they need to make the 'fresh start' that the juvenile justice system promises?

On 6 May 2020, we woke up to the report of a 16-year-old boy who had jumped off the fourteenth floor of his apartment complex. Just before that he was sitting at the dinner table with his parents. It emerged that a girl his age had posted on Instagram that she had been molested by him when he was 14 years old. As is to be expected, the trolling began with him being called a molester, abuser and even a rapist. The story went viral on social media platforms—after all, all it takes is the swish of a finger! We will never know the truth of these allegations, since the boy is dead. But it was shame and fear of punishment that led to his suicide. Under the Protection of Children from Sexual Offences (POCSO) Act, 2012, any sexual interaction before the age of 18 years amounts to a sexual offence.

Just a little before that the other story that made headlines was called the #BoisLockerRoom—again on Instagram. The misogynistic and violent language used in the chat group became the topic of media discussion. The chairperson of the Delhi Commission for Women, known for her demands for punitive action, jumped in. She wanted all the young people associated with the post to be arrested and punished. That would have meant those who posted the pictures and the comments, as well as those who liked and forwarded them— all would need to be apprehended and punished. They would all have to be placed in the system. It was rumoured and reported that some had been 'picked up' for questioning. As with all such sensational news, nothing more was heard of it.

But was that the solution? Would that have stopped cyber-bullying, stalking and shaming?

Contrary to populist perception that all of us who work with young offenders believe that they must not be punished, we do believe children who offend must be held accountable and brought into system. But we also believe that simply enhancing punitive measures, which involves long incarcerations, is not the solution. What they need is psycho-social support to recognize the harm they have caused and the consequences of their actions to the people they have harmed. They must recognize that they need to be accountable for their actions and that the only reason they are in the system is because they are underage and the legal system is willing and designed to provide them with an opportunity to reform—to give them a fresh start.

Unfortunately, the juvenile justice system as it exists has little support for children, and even less for those who work with the CICL. In many ways it is a broken system, understaffed and run by people who do not care. They are not the best trained nor the most competent. They often lead lives filled with challenges themselves, and have unresolved psychological issues from their own past, perhaps making it harder to be compassionate to the boys and girls who don't always lend themselves to affection by their rude, aggressive and often violent behaviour. In most homes or institutions, the superintendent may come and go, but the lower rung of staff—the caretakers, the cooks and other support staff—continue, year after year, faceless and unrecognized for what they do. Yes, they get a salary, but what else is done to keep them motivated? How do they feel cared for? Or recognized for what they do. The attitudes of both the children and the system do not inspire them to do more. The only time they come to the limelight is if children escape. Then they are the ones to be blamed, chargesheeted and suspended or dismissed.

Is it any surprise then that these caregivers become apathetic and hardened? Even as parents we sometimes feel overwhelmed and exhausted. And in their case, these are children who often come with a whole bunch of behavioural and emotional problems that can seem unresolvable.

It doesn't help that most who are part of the juvenile justice system are 'posted' in it. It's their job. And not an awfully pleasant one at that. Most treat it as a punishment posting. Only those who love all children of all ages unconditionally will find this work rewarding. But that is utopia. Should there not be self-care programmes, capacity building programmes, and recognition beyond the usual promotion and salary raise for these caregivers?

This book is about children who offend—some who mend and reform, and others who do not. Those who do not cannot be the reason why we must not continue to work with all those others who need our support and can and do make a fresh start. And for that we must keep reminding ourselves of all those children who did make a fresh start—who never returned to the 'system'.

Most struggle on their own and 'grow out of it', with very little support from us. They no longer feel the need to break the law or offend. Perhaps, if they had received a little support, they may have been able to make this transition more easily. Testimonies of children from all over the world exemplify this. I know from my own experience how hopeless and difficult the situation can sometimes appear.

What makes it harder is that we cannot change the circumstances the children go back to after we have helped them successfully negotiate the system or, if needed, fight it. They go right back to the same circumstances that had made them vulnerable to becoming offenders in the first place. The same influences. It's a recipe for turning them into 'repeaters'.

Dr Kalpana Purushothaman, who has herself been a member of a Juvenile Justice Board, in Karnataka, sums up the general ignorance of and indifference to the plight of these children in a crisp and incisive phrase—'the blindness of privilege'. 'When we come from privilege, we are unable to understand the lives of many of these children who lie to stay alive, steal for their lives to go on, children for whom drugs become more important than food. Our privilege often prevents us from seeing, acknowledging and understanding lives or experiences different from our own,' is how she put it to me in one of our long conversations. It is thus of utmost importance to keep reminding ourselves of the many factors that bring these children into the system—not as a justification for their crime, but to build our understanding and to prevent them from happening.

Shantha Sinha, who has been a child rights advocate for over thirty years, echoes this sentiment. She was the first chairperson of the National Commission for Protection of Child Rights (NCPCR) when it was set up on 5 March 2007 and served in that capacity for two terms. Shantha has throughout never ceased to remind us that it is not the children who are in conflict with the law, it is the state and its institutions which are. In her opinion, it is only the state that has to be held accountable for its dereliction of duty towards children, and not the children.

Even to categorize children under the juvenile justice system as Children in Conflict with Law and Children in Need of Care and Protection is, according to Shantha, a false dichotomy. In doing so, the child is held responsible for misbehaviour and the state's inaction to protect the child is totally ignored. Children cannot, no matter what, she believes, be held responsible for their circumstances of poverty, marginalization, deprivation and, consequently, for their state of being in 'conflict with the law'. According to her it is the state's constitutional duty to ensure that justice is meted out to these children.

'Is it not the state that has harmed children by not meeting its obligation to guarantee their fundamental right to equality, education, food and life with dignity at every step in their lives? Is it not the failure of the state to abide by the laws of the land that the child finds itself on "the other side of law?",' she asks.

It is she who brought my attention to an interesting, and telling, phenomenon. For all of us who work with the juvenile justice system, it is the 'institution'—the Observation Home, Special Home, the Children's Home—that has been our entry point. Because, as Shantha points out, these institutions are a mirror of society and all that is wrong in it. The children experience the violence and discrimination that pervades society much more intensely in the microcosm of the 'institution', and their plight offers a window to a reality which many among us remain comfortably oblivious to.

Shantha's sentiments find resonance in the opening lines of a paper by Stephen Wizner, Clinical Professor Emeritus of Law, Yale Law School, on the juvenile justice system: 'When the child and the state confront each other in the juvenile justice system, no amount of benevolent intentions, studied informality, or euphemistic terminology should be allowed to obscure the fact that they are, in fact, adversaries. What is at stake in juvenile delinquency proceedings is the child's right to liberty and his right to continue in the custody of his parents against the state's power to control crime and enforce morality.'[14]

This book is thus equally about people who have worked with these children. It's only hope that keeps us going. And I know that for myself. There have been times when I too have found it very hard to dip into myself and find compassion within for the young offender, knowing he was responsible for some egregious acts (rape and murder, sodomy, etc.). And I know many others like me who have struggled in like manner. What gives us hope are the hundreds and thousands of children that stand testimony to the fact that, with a second chance and just a little bit of support, young people who may have crossed over to the other side of the law, can and do 'reform'.

1

OFFENDER OR VICTIM?

I was watching writer and activist Kimberley Latrice Jones[1] say of the looting that took place in the USA during the Black Lives Matter protests, 'Economic disadvantage allows you to brutalize people.' My mind went back to a conversation with a police officer I had met many years ago.

We were in a police station on the outskirts of Delhi. The training session had just finished. Over a cup of tea with the DCP,[2] we got talking about the higher rate of juvenile crimes in 'his area', which also happened to be the home of many on the margins of society.

'Madam, just think about this. Do you see those big malls with all those huge shop windows? These poor boys walk past them every day and see those beautiful displays. They know they can never afford those things. They will never be allowed to step inside that mall. So, one day one of them picks up a stone and hurls it at the glass. He becomes a child in conflict with the law. But is he really a criminal? Can we really blame him? These are the boys I meet every day. Madam, the message to them is: All this is available, but not for you…'

This conversation stayed with me. One day when Aseem

(name changed) came to the office for his regular counselling, looking petulant and bored, I walked in to sit with him and his counsellor. He was fidgety and non-communicative. He had admitted that he had been with the boys who had gang raped '*that* girl'. But he insisted that while he was high on drugs like the others, he had not participated in the assault. Besides this he would not say anything. I had watched him come for all the slated sessions in the past—walk in and walk out with the same expression. The counsellor too had reached a dead end. That day, on a whim, I had walked inside. My children say I can talk to a tree. So, there I was, facing Aseem, with his shut expression. My questions brought monosyllabic responses. When I asked him where he lived, and he named the place, I asked, 'Isn't that next to a mall?'

He suddenly perked up. 'Yes, it's a really big mall and it's quite close to my house.'

'Have you been there?'

'No. Never.'

'Would you like to go?'

'They will never allow me in.'

'What if the *bhaiyas* and *didis* from here went with you? Let's plan a visit.' (The children often refer to the counsellors as *Bhaiya* [brother] or *Didi* [sister].)

Aseem was excited. The date was fixed. Two of HAQ's counsellors picked Aseem and his sisters dressed in their best clothes and went to the mall. At the gate the guard stopped them. He looked at the counsellors and said, 'You can go in. These children cannot.'

'Why can't they?'

'They cannot afford anything in there. They will make a nuisance of themselves.'

'How do you know they don't have the money? And

how do you know they will make a nuisance of themselves? They have the money. Besides, they are with us and we have enough.'

'No. They cannot go in. The other customers will object and I will lose my job. *Please aap log bahas mat karo.*' (Please do not argue unnecessarily.)

A small group had gathered. Aseem and his sisters tugged at the counsellor's hand and said, '*Chalo! Humein pata tha woh humein andar nahin jaane denge.*' (Let's go. We knew they wouldn't let us in.)

The counsellors told me what had happened. They were very offended. But Aseem was not. He was stoic—at least at that moment. He was only too aware that his economic disadvantage allows his brutalization by others. He was already a child in conflict with the law, a child in the system. Who knows when he too will turn into the young person the police officer had described? The one who hurled the stone. He is of course not the only one. He was only one of the few we had access to.

All this came back to me again as I read G.S. Bajpai's book on juvenile justice in which he writes: 'They desire to participate in the process of upward mobility witnessed in some parts of the country but lack the opportunities to do so. Above all, they strive to become part of a society that continually fails nourish them with enriching lives. Such aspirations and strife in young and adolescent minds, largely ill-equipped to handle them, produce conflict...'[3]

While delivering a judgement in 2019, Justice D.S. Naidu of the Bombay High Court prefaced it by invoking William Shakespeare: 'In Winter's Tale (Act 3, Scene 3), through a shepherd, he bemoans the terrible teens: I would that there were no age between sixteen and three-and-twenty, or that youth would sleep out the rest, for there is nothing in the between but getting wenches with child, wronging the ancientry, stealing, fighting...'[4] What was reality then, in the times of William Shakespeare, remains so even today.

A study titled *Juvenile in Conflict with the Law and Administration of Juvenile Justice System in States of Maharashtra and Rajasthan*[5] commissioned by the National Commission for Protection of Child Rights (NCPCR) and conducted by the Tata Institute of Social Sciences (TISS), Mumbai, verifies the belief that crimes committed by children are the result of an interplay of several factors at the level of the individual, the family, the neighbourhood, the community and society at large. While the study indicates that there is no one identical profile of juveniles or any uniform family characteristics, it identifies the factors responsible for child crime to be economic, educational and familial and age-peer equation related. It also points to the lack of adult monitoring, supervision and guidance, improper environment (school, family, neighbourhood and workplace), addiction, inadequate daily living conditions (be it facilities and amenities at home and school or human relationships with trusting and caring adults) and the neglect of the mental health of children as the foremost reasons.

The study shows a majority of the children apprehended to be first-time offenders, between 16 and 18 years of age, from lower socio-economic backgrounds, equipped with middle-school education (92 per cent) with continued enrolment (46 per cent) and living with families (97.1 per cent). These children face conflict at home (14 per cent) and addiction (40 per cent), witness fights in the neighbourhood (54 per cent), have been caught largely for theft and robbery, and were apprehended with friends (59 per cent).

Other studies point to easy access to weapons as well as alcohol and other substances, poor police presence in the slums or colonies the children live in and the adverse influence of films and the media as noteworthy causes.[6]

Another study, by legal scholars B.R. Sharma, Sangeet Dhillon and Sarmadi Bano, identifies individual factors or personality traits like submissiveness, defiance, hostility, impulsiveness, insecurity, fear, lack of self-control and emotional conflicts and situational factors like family, companions, movies, school environment and work environment as causes for children's criminality.[7]

In a paper titled *Counselling Children in Conflict with the Law: Experiences and Lessons* (2012; updated in 2014), based on counselling provided to children in an Observation Home in Delhi, HAQ identified poverty; inadequate living spaces; high drop-out rates from schools (due to overcrowding, violence, poor quality of teaching and corporal punishment); lack of family structure and support; the family's inattention to children's psychological needs and their deviations (like substance abuse and criminal behaviour); children's poor understanding of responsible actions and behaviour; an absence of avenues for vocational training and recreational outlets; and a lack of conversations or sensitization to issues of sexuality as major reasons for children committing crime.

As can be seen, the prime causes behind children committing crimes are replicated in study after study with disturbing regularity. While it is true that not all poor people take to crime, it is equally true that being on the lower rungs of the socio-economic pecking order does make them more vulnerable to being drawn into it. It is pertinent to note that 42.4 per cent CICL came from families whose annual income is Rs 25,000 or below, according to the *Crime in*

India 2015 statistics of the National Crime Records Bureau (NCRB). For Delhi the figure was 53.5 per cent of the CICL. (Family income was provided till 2015. This data is not provided in subsequent reports.) According to Saju Parackal and Rita Panicker, who work among street and working children and have written about children in conflict with the law in India: 'Data shows that offending/deviance is an issue prevalent in all socio-economic classes of people but only those from the lower classes are likely to be incarcerated, charged or convicted. The evidences and experiences strongly contest the premise that poverty is the root cause of all offending behaviour… However, this does not mean that all deviant/offending acts of children delink itself from the influence of poverty/economic strain but emphasize that it is not an exclusive factor but a distant risk factor for juvenile deviance.'[8]

Given the triggers for offending, data as well as anecdotal evidence confirm that it is the marginalized who are far more likely to enter the system and remain within it. Both the privileged child as well as the hungry child can be picked up by the police based on their actions. But it is those on the margins who remain far more vulnerable to the 'long arms of justice'. And this is true even in developed countries like the USA, where it is the Black and ethnic minority children that make up the disproportionate number within the system.[9] And just as the great majority of children apprehended for crimes in the USA are Black, in Australia, they are aboriginal youth. A report by the Productivity Commission, an advisory body of the Australian government, for example, tells us that aboriginal children (10–17 years) had been detained twenty-three times more than non-Indigenous young people in the justice system nationally in 2018–19.[10]

In the USA, as far back as the 1940s, a report by sociologist Mary Huff Diggs had documented the phenomenon of disproportionate minority contact (DMC) in youth court cases. In her review of fifty-three courts across the country, she identified 'that Negro children are represented in a much larger proportion of the delinquency cases than they are in the general population'. Additionally, she noted 'cases of Negro boys were less frequently dismissed than those of White boys. Besides, they were committed to an institution or referred to an agency or individual much more frequently than were White boys'.[11] Indeed, Diggs's DMC findings highlighted the deep-rooted disproportionality problem that continues to plague the youth justice system in the USA even today.[12]

In an article on *Juvenile Justice Information Exchange*, American legal practitioners Buta Biberaj, Carol Siemon and Miriam Krinsky write, 'America incarcerates *more people under 18*[13] than any other nation and is the *only country in the world*[14] to condemn its children to die behind bars, with no chance of freedom or hope for redemption. For these "juvenile lifers", no matter their progress in treatment or rehabilitation, their home from the age of 15—or whenever they were sentenced as a child—is a jail cell.'[15] They add that the system perpetuates unconscionable racial inequities. The majority of these 'juvenile life without parole' (JLWOP) sentences are given to Black individuals. 'The system is sadly predisposed to see the humanity in white children more than children of colour; approximately *70% of children sentenced to life without parole have been Black* since 2012.'[16]

What is more, the shrill narratives around juvenile offenders that we witness in India are mirrored in the USA. Just as we saw in the case of the juvenile in the Nirbhaya case, often in the US too, a devastating narrative gets created around the proclivity of 'black boys' to commit such horrible crimes.

Tracing the history of the 'youth of colour in the justice system', James Bell of the W. Haywood Burns Institute for Juvenile Justice Fairness and Equity notes how, in the Central Park Jogger case, for example, young men of colour had been described as 'animals' roaming in 'feral packs'.[17] This particular incident took place 1989, in which a young woman was brutally sexually assaulted when she was out jogging in New York's Central Park. Five boys of colour between the ages of 14 and 16 were tried and convicted in a highly publicized trial despite an absence of physical evidence and incoherent, and recanted, confessions.

The boys were pronounced deserving of harsher and more punitive treatment. Not surprisingly, these teenage boys were incarcerated for nearly thirteen years for a crime they did not commit. The five convictions were ultimately overturned in 2002 when the actual attacker confessed and was linked to the crime by DNA evidence.[18] As Jim Dwyer wrote in the *New York Times*, 'Locking up those boys for a gang rape that had not happened but that most of society believed in was the same as planting a bomb in their lives that never stopped exploding.'[19]

But the stereotyping of certain groups and their proclivity towards violence persists. And hence they continue to be disproportionately represented in the 'system'. The situation differs merely in the particulars across continents.

I will have to admit that before I began interacting with children who had offended, I was just as influenced by the pre-conceived notions that afflict the rest of society. Just like most people, I expected *those* children to look and behave differently. And so, like Puneeta Roy, who describes (in Part 2 of this book) how, when she first set foot in an Observation Home, she found that the children she saw there looked 'no different from the hundreds of young adults I have worked with…in private and government schools across Delhi', I too went through a period of shedding the various misconceptions that clouded my judgement.

Unfortunately, as the offences, in all their gory voyeuristic detail, are described by the media, each one of us finds it harder and harder to focus on the offender. The offence defines the offender and by extension shapes our opinion of the person. And so, most of us find it easy to declare and believe that if these children can commit an offence of this nature, they are mature enough to understand its implications as well. It is a forgone conclusion. We forget their circumstances, the fact that they may have been young and impulsive, the peer pressure they must face and often the dark past they may have lived through—or continue to live through. And so, when actually confronted with a child in conflict with the law, or a child *offender*, and when our presuppositions are thus challenged, the first reaction is surprise.

The journey from living comfortably with our pre-conceived notions to empathy is what defines the journey of those who work with children who offend.

Although I had been visiting a Children's Home that housed neglected and abandoned children since 1993, my actual interaction with children who *offend* began in the 2000s, a few years after I co-founded HAQ. The storyline is clear, but the timelines are a bit muddled. It was so long ago.

It all began with a phone call. Bharti Ali, my co-director then, called to say that Ramesh (name changed), the 16-year-old son of her domestic help had been picked up by the police in the middle of the night from a slum colony and his mother could not find him. The family had rushed to the police station, but the police would not cooperate.

Bharti called 100 (the national emergency helpline number for police) and helped the woman file a missing child complaint. When there was no news of the child, a habeas corpus petition was filed and the child was produced in court. The police version was that a theft had been reported and so the boy was picked up for 'pooch tach' (questioning).

But the boy's version, when we finally met him, was different. His brother had fallen into bad company and his friends were thieves. On that particular night, based on a complaint of theft received by them, the police had come looking for Ramesh's brother. Since the brother was not at home, they took Ramesh away and put him in lock-up. Realizing that they had perhaps made a mistake, they beat Ramesh up, put a 'katta' (a country-made revolver) in his hand, beat him up again for having a gun, and booked him under the Arms Act. Then they shifted him to Tihar Jail and there he stayed till he was produced in the High Court following the habeas corpus petition. After much back and forth and examination of his age, he was placed in an Observation Home for Boys (OHB).[20] Following several hearings in the Juvenile Justice Board (JJB), and no evidence against him, Ramesh was sent back home.

This case marked the beginning of HAQ's, and my own, journey on juvenile justice. The habeas corpus case was heard by Justice Madan B. Lokur (he was then a judge in the Delhi High Court). Little did he know that this case would actually be his introduction to the world of juvenile justice, which was to become his special area of interest a few years on, particularly once he was designated the chairperson of the Juvenile Justice Committee of the Delhi High Court. He has remained a passionate advocate for juvenile justice ever since. His experiences are part of this book too.

Recognizing how children languish in Observation Homes without legal representation, we began to provide legal aid to children who had offended. In turn, we too gained insights into the lives of young boys and girls. After some time, the Principal Magistrate heading the JJB in Delhi asked us if HAQ could provide counselling to the children. There really was no one else! So we agreed. This brought HAQ directly into the lives of these children. It enabled us to visit the children in the OHB, interact with them and understand them better. Many of our interactions with these children also took place in the *kharja*, which is the name given to the waiting hall.

The usual practice is that a JJB is located close to, or on the premises of an OHB. Just before the hearing, the children are brought from the OHB, or any other facility where they are being held (like the Special Home or Place of Safety[21]), and placed in the *kharja*. This is where they wait until they are called in for their hearing by the JJB. After the hearing, if not released on bail or acquitted, they are sent back to the child care facility where they are housed. To give an analogy, it is the equivalent to lockups in courts where the undertrials are placed before being produced in court when it is their turn.

Every visit to the OHB was a mixed experience. It was overcrowded, filled with children who were awaiting bail. Some of the boys were pure delight—despite their confinement, they were filled with hope and energy. Then there were the angry or petulant macho ones who looked at us with disdain

and arrogance as we tried to make conversation. A peculiar smell—a combination of hair oils, dampness and body odour from sweaty, unwashed bodies—hung in the air. Combined with this was the smell of the toilets. The windows were all barred, and there was scarcely any sunlight. The walls were greasy and marked by dirty hands and oil from heads as boys leaned on them.

The experience of visiting the *kharja* was on another level altogether. In fact, the first time was quite a shock. Through a heavily grilled window, we heard boys loudly calling out to us. To talk to the boys, one had to go very close to the grill, where there were several noses stuck against it. Some of them were cheeky. But behind their cheekiness was hesitation and we could sense the fear in their eyes as they waited uncertainly for their hearings.

Although visits to the Observation Home for Girls (OHG) are much less frequent, the overall feeling and environment is not very different. Only the numbers accommodated in the facility is much smaller. The look of desperation and hopelessness in the eyes of the girls is only too familiar.

In 2007, Ruzbeh Bharucha joined us as a volunteer and began visiting the different institutions which apprehended children found themselves in. I too would accompany him on some of those visits. Based on his interactions with the children he wrote *My God is a Juvenile Delinquent* (2008). The book is a poignant account of the emotional and psychological issues they face and documents how the lives of these children lead them to crime.

Now every time I visit a children's institution, Ruzbeh's words come rushing back to me. 'After having visited a number of prisons, orphanages, Observation Homes and shelter homes, I have come to the conclusion that we Indians put in great thought and a conscious effort to make our institutions dreary, depressing, suffocating and try our best to block and keep out stuff like sunlight, air and cross ventilation,' he writes.[22] Even his observation about 'the most horrid mish-mash of colours on the walls' resonates with mine. I have often wondered why it is that the colours are dark and drab. I have concluded in my own head, since no one has ever explained to me the actual reason, that they just repeat what was there earlier and simply paint over, if they do so at all. Moreover, with the children dirtying the walls, the dark colours perhaps help better camouflage the dirt and goop. After all, it's usually many years before the walls are repainted.

Divya Srivastava, a Mumbai-based counsellor and psychiatrist describes these places as 'hell holes rather than reform centres'. As she says, 'In most special homes or observation homes, around 12 to 20 children share a room. The rooms are usually small and feel crammed due to overcrowding. There is no privacy, and as the spaces are cramped, levels of irritation and annoyance are high, because someone or the other is always around to create a certain level of disturbance. Overcrowding often leads to violent fights over trivial issues.'[23]

We once met a 16-year-old staring at us through the wire mesh of the *kharja* and asked him why he was there. He replied, 'Murder. Another man was with me and actually he was the one who murdered. I was just an onlooker.' He added that he had been in the OHB since he was 14 years old. The 'man' was in jail and had been charged for life. But he could not understand why he continued to be 'jailed'. He kept saying, 'It's been two and a half years and nobody seems to be bothered about me.'

Ruzbeh described our apprehensions vividly. 'He looked sixteen, had a gangly beard which had never made contact with a razor, wore clean clothes, looked like the thousands of boys who roam around various markets and cinema halls and the ubiquitous malls that have mushroomed all over the country. For some reason, I didn't believe he was completely innocent. To doubt a boy of sixteen of committing murder or assisting in committing a murder made me feel wretched. If he had committed the crime, what a burden to carry all through life: what a heavy cross to bear. But if he was really innocent, how was anybody going to be able to recompense lost childhood. That's a price nobody can afford to pay or lose.'[24]

Sunny, as the boy called himself, was in the Observation Home because no one really cared that he was locked up for over two years. No one came to visit him or apply for his bail. Any guesses what this lost child, filled with angst, will be like when he is finally discharged? How will he handle his anger and his anxieties, his feeling of being abandoned? In the absence of any support, will he end up in the world of crime?

The 'system' is a quagmire that many find it very hard to pull themselves out of. The system does not help. If anything, the apathy of the system—the overcrowded spaces, the lack of anything to engage the young minds, the stigma of being a 'criminal' or 'offender', or 'juvenile'—a word that has become synonymous with 'juvenile delinquent'—makes it nigh impossible to get back to a 'normal' life. Even a cursory look at India's crime records can help us gauge the scale of the problem. According to the *Crime in India 2021* report of the National Crime Records Bureau, for example, 40,288 cases involving children that were pending since the previous year. With 37,444 more children apprehended in the beginning of 2021 in addition to the backlog of pending cases, a total of 77,732 children needed to be heard by the already overburdened courts. By the end of 2021, 40,519 children's cases (52.1 per cent) were still pending.[25]

Throughout history, the challenge has been one of figuring out what the right age is when a child can be considered 'grown up enough'—when does childhood end? When can one be grown up enough to have sex, be married or go to work? Of course, an answer to this question also determines the consequences of one's actions and, in particular, the severity of punishment in the case of an offence being committed. Social norms and legal definitions have evolved over centuries, and the debate has continued.

Many of us have seen shifts in the concept of childhood in our own lifetimes. When my grandmother was married off at 11 years, she was definitely thought of as old enough to be married and take on household responsibilities. But by the time my mother was born, 11 was much too young to be married. The earliest any of her siblings got married was at the age of 18 years. My mother married at 29, which, though no longer young, was still all right to be married at. Nobody expected her to marry before 18 years. Childhood in my own family was thus extended. And our experience has been similar to the change that has taken place across societies around the globe.

At some point, the globally agreed upon cut-off point in international law for the end of childhood was set at 18 years (unless, under the law applicable, majority is attained earlier).[26] When they reach 18 years, individuals are deemed legally responsible for their actions and the consequences of

those actions. It is true that this sudden cut-off of 18 years may seem arbitrary—and many people do say so. 'How can you treat a person who is 17 years and 364 days as a child, and the moment they cross the threshold of 18 years, as an adult?' they ask. 'Does their capacity for acting responsibly change so fundamentally in a matter of a day?' In fact, that was the very question being asked regarding the 'juvenile' in the Nirbhaya case.

'Legal line drawing is inevitably arbitrary at the margins,' assert Elizabeth S. Scott and Laurence Steinberg, leading authorities on juvenile justice and adolescence, respectively, which unfortunately means that there is a standard set of punishments for legal adults, whether 18 or 38. But the default age of majority is still set at 18 years, since it '*seems like a natural dividing line between adult and juvenile status in the justice system*' (emphasis added).[27] This cut-off age of 18 is especially arbitrary since we now know that the development of the human brain continues till the mid-twenties.

As Penal Reform International points out, 'There is no formal rite of passage from the status of supervised childhood to autonomous and morally responsible adulthood… However, the important point about setting an age of majority is that it creates uniformity.'[28] In fact, in all my research, I could not find anything that explained to me when, why and how the age of 18 years was arrived at. Even before India ratified the United Nations Convention on the Rights of the Child (UNCRC) of 1989, only those over 18 could sign a contract or drive a car, similar to most countries of the world. (Some, like the USA, allow it at 16 years in some States.)

Despite the existence of the concept of juvenile justice for over a century, the debate on how an 'offending child must be treated' continues. It isn't hard to imagine a lack of self-awareness among many people who might call for severe retribution for someone else's child, on the one hand, and on the other argue vehemently to the contrary if it is their own child who is found to have broken the law, insisting that they are children and were likely behaving impulsively, as children do. But a similar lack of consistency can be seen at an institutional level as well.

On 4 May 2021, at a session in preparation for the World Congress on Justice for Children (which was held in November of that year), I was invited to interact with young people who had been in contact with the law. Sharing their experiences, one of them made a very astute and insightful observation: 'There is always a tendency to "adultify" children's behaviour. This is why the knee-jerk reaction is to treat them under the adult justice system.'

Therein lies the contradiction. The juvenile justice system is supposed to adopt a child-friendly approach. This inherently means it must be adapted to the circumstances of the child—one of which is age and evolving capacity.

But while we find that it often treats children as adults—adult time for adult crime being the logic—we do on occasion find that the system can simultaneously 'infantilize' the children when it comes to the facilities it provides. A most obvious example of this is that a child-friendly environment is interpreted by many of those in positions of authority as pink walls with cartoons painted on them! It's seldom understood in terms of listening to and respecting the views of children. As a result, this already vulnerable group of children must suffer the worst of both worlds.

Societal notions of childhood and responsibility have been defined and redefined throughout history and in turn have

influenced our understanding of what constitutes juvenile justice. As historian Pat Thane notes, 'Most of the divergences in the ages at which children acquire adult responsibilities in the worlds of work, crime, politics, sex and other activities, and the assumed slower acquisition by girls than boys of some but not other aspects of adult competence reflect historical changes in definitions of childhood. The statutes which enforce them often express the view prevailing at the time of the enactment.'[29]

The famous French historian and medievalist Philippe Aries traced the historical changes that occurred in the construction and understanding of childhood. According to him, it was only in the sixteenth and seventeenth centuries that the consciousness of the specific nature of childhood, as distinct from infancy and adulthood, emerged. Prior to this, the awareness of what differentiates a child and an adult was largely missing.[30] Aries was not suggesting that families did not love their children, or show affection to them, but that childhood was not recognized or valued as a distinct phase.[31] His observations were of course based completely on his study of Western societies, but they do find some resonance in India too where one has continuously witnessed, often within a lifetime, changes in notions about childhood. Even today, such notions vary with class or cultural norms. The children of the poor, for example, are forced to take on 'adult roles' much earlier than their privileged counterparts.

However, what remains universal across all cultures is the fact that the largest number of crimes are not committed by very young children. They are by persons who are going through adolescence—the phase of life that stretches between childhood and adulthood.[32] This period usually begins at the age of 10. While some consider adolescence to coincide with

10–19 years, there are also those who suggest that it may stretch further beyond. But in the context of juvenile justice, 18 is the agreed upon age across most countries of the world.

What is also established is that adolescence is a phase marked by increased experimentation, risk taking, a tendency to discount long-term consequences, heightened sensitivity to peers and other social influences. Much of the adolescent involvement in illegal activity is an extension of this very risk-taking behaviour—a part of the developmental process of identity formation. That is why we find adolescents experimenting with drugs, unsafe sex, reckless driving and aggressive behaviour that may even turn violent. Research has also shown that this risky experimentation, for the majority of people, does not extend beyond adolescence. It ceases as identity becomes settled with maturity.[33]

The reality is that most of us exhibit some of these characteristics to varying degrees as we grow up. Some of our 'experimentation', if caught, could have resulted in being treated as criminal activity and we would have crossed over to becoming children in conflict with the law. We were simply lucky.

It is the recognition of factors that lead to *some* adolescents coming into conflict with the law, and their capacity to reform and make a fresh start as responsible citizens, that forms—and must form—the foundation of the juvenile justice system. The underlying premise, therefore, of treating children and young people differently when they come into conflict with the law is that they are more susceptible to positive influence than adults, and hence more likely to change their behaviour.

Indeed, the overarching goal of juvenile justice systems across the world remains to develop pro-social development of the young individuals who come into the system, to

support them to reform and reintegrate into regular life. The aim is simultaneously also to hold them accountable for their wrongdoing, treat them fairly and prevent them from re-offending or sliding into adult offending, and thereby ensuring the safety of communities. It follows from the belief that punitive measures do not address the root causes of offending, can arrest children's development, can blow them off course leading to their life chances being diminished, which may, in turn, lead to increased re-offending.[34]

Thus, both preventing crime by children and protecting them from becoming victims of crime are central to protecting children's rights. It is the recognition of this important fact that forms the bedrock of the juvenile justice system in India, which has, at least at the *level of policy*, always adopted a welfarist model that has both a preventive and curative aspect to it and has always addressed two categories of children—Children in Conflict with the Law (CICL) and Children in Need of Care and Protection (CNCP), i.e. children who may be vulnerable to offending because of their circumstances.

At a conference organized by the Judicial Academy of Odisha in April 2022, Justice Harish Tandon of the High Court of Calcutta described the purpose of juvenile justice as 'correction with compassion'. That is one of the best summing-up phrases on the purpose of the juvenile justice system that I have heard.

2

THE ANATOMY OF THE LAW

A special law to address children who may have offended, or were vulnerable to offending, is a part of India's colonial legacy, brought in by the British rulers. The first legislation, the Apprentice Act that came in 1850, provided that children in the age group of 10–18 convicted by courts be provided with some vocational training which might help in their rehabilitation. It was followed eventually by the Reformatory Schools Act, 1897.

The Indian Jails Committee report (1919–20), which recommended the need for trial and treatment of young offenders within a system separate from adults, was an important milestone in the evolution of juvenile justice in India. The Jails Committee report noted: 'The first impulse towards reform came in this matter, as in many others, from America. It was in that country that the first children's court was called into existence and it is in America that the theory of the State's responsibility towards the child has been most fully developed.'

In this context it is ironical that the USA has not ratified the Convention on the Rights of the Child (UNCRC) and also continued to have capital punishment for children till

2004. On 27 January 2004, the Supreme Court of the United States of America decided to review whether executing 16- and 17-year-olds violates the Constitution's ban on 'cruel and unusual punishment'. The review came after the Missouri Supreme Court overturned the death sentence of 17-year-old Christopher Simmons in *Roper vs Simmons*. In March 2005, the US Supreme Court ruled that standards of decency have evolved such that executing juvenile offenders who committed crimes while younger than 18 is 'cruel and unusual punishment' prohibited by the Eighth Amendment.[1] But it continues to permit the punishment of life sentence without parole.[2]

The Jails Committee report further said:

In no direction have more important changes been effected in the last thirty years than in the treatment of the child-offender. Until nearly the close of the last century, children, if over the age of seven, were not regarded or dealt with by the criminal courts very differently from adults. They were tried in the same courts and with the same procedures, sentenced to similar penalties and imprisoned in the same prisons; but these views are no longer the sole property of any one country. It is now generally recognized that the ordinary healthy child criminal is mainly the product of unfavourable environment and that he is entitled to a fresh chance under better surroundings. There is a general consensus of the opinion that as youth is the time when habits have not become fixed, the prospects of reformation are then most hopeful. From both points of view it has come to be agreed that the child offender should be given different treatment from the adult.

Given the debates that India has witnessed over the last few years regarding the need for children to be punished according to the gravity of the offence they commit and not their age, what the Jails Committee said in 1920 appears so much more progressive!

Its recommendations prompted the enactment of the Children Act in Madras in 1920, where the first Children's Court was established.[3] This was followed by the Bengal and Bombay Acts in 1922 and 1924, respectively. All this happened in pre-Independence India, when the country was divided into Madras, Bombay and Bengal, which began as Presidencies and were then made into Provinces, along with several others. These three pioneering statutes (i.e. the Acts in Madras, Bengal and Bombay) were extensively amended between 1948 and 1959, after Independence. The Children Act, 1960 (Act No. 60 dated 26 December 1960) extended the provisions of these laws to all Union Territories.[4]

All the Children Acts were similar and addressed both delinquent and neglected children. Just as is the case with the present law for juvenile justice in India, the reason for inclusion of these two categories of children was aimed at both protection and rehabilitation—protecting them from harm and preventing neglected and vulnerable children from falling into delinquency by providing them the necessary support. These Acts permitted imprisonment of children in cases of a serious offence. 'Child' was defined as a boy who had not attained the age of 16 years or a girl who had not attained the age of 18 years. They were housed in an Observation Home during the trial and if convicted sent to a special school. But there was no pan-India Act to govern children and the States[5] had to enact their own legislation. The Act of 1960, as mentioned above, covered only Union Territories.

In this law, the Children's Welfare Board consisted of a

chairman and such other members as the administrator of the Union territory thought fit to appoint, of whom not less than one was to be a woman. Just as it is now the case with the Child Welfare Committee,[6] the powers vested with the Board (as a whole) were that of a magistrate under the Code of Criminal Procedure, 1973. The Children's Court consisted of such number of metropolitan magistrates or judicial magistrates, forming a bench, as the government thought fit to appoint, of whom one was designated as the Principal Magistrate. Every such bench had the powers conferred by the Code of Criminal Procedure, 1973 on a metropolitan magistrate or a judicial magistrate. Every Children's Court was to be assisted by a panel of two honorary social workers. In many ways, as we shall see, it remains a precursor to the law we have today—addressing both neglected as well as delinquent children, with the provision of a board that included at least one woman, and also social workers. Of course, there are terminologies that have changed over time.

The first national law on juvenile justice was enacted in 1986 as a result of the efforts and struggles of a journalist named Sheela Barse. In 1983, Sheela Barse filed a habeas corpus writ petition in public interest in the Supreme Court of India for the release of 1,400 children who, as per official records of the government, were in prisons. She claimed that these children were illegally confined as the Children Acts of various States prohibited keeping of children in prisons. The Supreme Court noted that it was primarily the differences in the Children Acts of various States that was resulting in differential treatment given to children in different States. The Supreme Court suggested to the Union of India that it should pass a uniform legislation for children across the territory of India to remove such inequality.[7] In its order in

Sheela Barse vs Union of India (13 August 1986) the Supreme Court observed as follows:

> We have by our order dated 5th August 1986 called upon the State Government to bring into force and to implement vigorously the provisions of the Children's Acts enacted in the various States. But we would suggest that instead of each State having its own Children's Act...it would be desirable if the Central Government initiates Parliamentary Legislation on the subject, so that there is complete uniformity in regard to the various provisions relating to children in the entire territory of the country. The Children's Act which may be enacted by Parliament should contain not only provisions for investigation and trial of offences against children below the age of 16 years but should also contain mandatory provisions for ensuring social, economic and psychological rehabilitation of the children who are either accused of offences or are abandoned or destitute or lost. Moreover, it is not enough merely to have legislation on the subject, but it is equally, if not more, important to ensure that such legislation is implemented in all earnestness and mere lip sympathy is not paid such legislation and justification for non-implementation is not pleaded on ground of lack of finances on the part of the State. The greatest recompense which the State can get for expenditure on children is the building up of a powerful human resource ready to take its place in the forward march of the nation.[8]

On 22 August 1986, the Juvenile Justice Bill, 1986 was introduced in the Lok Sabha. Like the Children Act, 1960, it defined a child as a person who hadn't yet attained the age of 18 years for girls and 16 years for boys. It became a law on 1 December 1986. The Juvenile Justice Act of 1986 (JJ Act, 1986) which applied uniformly to the whole of India,

except the State of Jammu and Kashmir, resolved some of the inconsistencies in legislation among various States. With the passage of this law, no child could be sent to prison or kept in a police station under any circumstance. The statement of objects and reasons of the JJ Act, 1986 stated:

> A review of the working of the existing Children Acts would indicate that much greater attention is required to be given to children who may be found in situations of social maladjustment, delinquency or neglect. The justice system as available for adults is not considered suitable for being applied to juveniles. It is also necessary that a uniform juvenile justice system should be available throughout the country which should make adequate provision for dealing with all aspects in the changing social, cultural and economic situation in the country. There is also need for larger involvement of informal systems and community-based welfare agencies in the care, protection, treatment, development and rehabilitation of such juveniles.

The above statement exemplifies the protective approach which continues to be observed in the contemporary Juvenile Justice (Care and Protection of Children) Act, 2000 (JJ Act, 2000), amended in 2006, and also in the 2015 (JJ Act, 2015) version. Crucially, in the JJ Act, 2000, the age of the child was raised to 18 years for both girls and boys.

In the JJ Act, 2015, a further provision for transfer of the child to be tried as an adult in certain serious offences was introduced on public demand, which shall be discussed in some detail later. Yet another set of amendments have been notified as this book goes to press towards the end of 2022.

Similar to the previous law, in the 1986 version of the JJ Act too there were two categories of children—juveniles (or CNCP in the 2000 version) and juvenile delinquents (or CICL in the 2000 version). Apprehended juveniles were produced before the Juvenile Board (now called the Child Welfare Committee, CWC[9]) and the Juvenile Court (now called the Juvenile Justice Board, JJB[10]).

Unlike in the current law, both categories of children (whether neglected juveniles or juvenile delinquents) under the 1986 version were first taken to an Observation Home or reception centre, and housed there till they were produced before the Juvenile Board or Juvenile Court. The Juvenile Board would, after addressing the situation of the neglected juvenile, decide if the child needed to be sent to a Juvenile Home. The Juvenile Court, after trial of the case, would decide if the child was to be sent to a Special Home or Place of Safety, which were institutional facilities for juvenile delinquents.

The Act of 2000 attempted to mitigate the stigma that is likely to result in the process. It requires that children in need of protection be brought directly to a Children's Home and be looked after by the Child Welfare Committee. A child caught committing an alleged offence, on the other hand, under the new law, has to be taken to a JJB and kept in an Observation Home while the child awaits judgement. If convicted by the JJB, those above 18 at the time of conviction are taken to a Place of Safety, and those below the age of 18 are taken to a Special Home.

Chapter 1 (Preliminary) of the JJ Act, 1986 explained that although the title of the JJ Act was formulated differently from that of the Children Act, 1960, there was no substantial difference in the provisions of the two enactments. The words 'maintenance', 'welfare', 'training', 'education' and 'trial', used in the Children Act, 1960 had been substituted by others such as 'care', 'protection', 'treatment', 'development and

rehabilitation' and 'adjudication' in the JJ Act. It is to be noted that the words 'treatment' and 'development' were more comprehensive than the words used in the Children Act, 1960. 'Treatment' provides reformative and rehabilitative orientation to the word 'training'. The object of the training for the juveniles under the Act was to reform the juveniles, to enable them to protect themselves against moral danger or exploitation and to rehabilitate them.[11]

Similarly, the word 'development' connotes a more integrated approach while providing maintenance, welfare, training and education. In order to minimize the social stigma attached to criminal prosecution, the Children Act, 1960 had avoided the use of criminal proceedings in its terminology. The JJ Act, 1986 says, 'The word "trial" was perhaps included in its long title [i.e. in the long title of the Children Act, 1960] by oversight. That error has now been corrected. Use of the words "adjudication and disposal of matters relating to juvenile delinquents" is in conformity with the non-criminal nature of the proceedings under the JJA.'[12]

The insertion of the words care and protection in the 1986 version is itself important, because they were included in the long title of the 2000 version as well. On this it says:

> The words 'care', 'protection' may be understood together as ensuring the well-being of the juveniles. While 'care' emphasizes the positive measures necessary for maintaining and looking after the juveniles in any reasonable manner, 'protection' aims at defending the juveniles from trouble, attack, harm, etc. The JJA aims to ensure the well-being of juveniles by positive as well as preventive measures. Various provisions contained in the JJA reflect the dual responsibility undertaken by the Act.

What is most important when either formulating or discussing laws for children is the recognition that children who come into contact with the law—as victims, witnesses, offenders or complainants—must meet with a system that understands and respects both their rights and their unique vulnerability.[13] A child-friendly justice is one that embraces the idea that courts can be a powerful tool to positively shape children's lives while recognizing that contact with the legal system is often a source of additional trauma than a remedy for children.[14] It is precisely the reason why we need laws and systems that mitigate the challenge of going through the legal proceedings for children, so that they can have confidence in the justice system. It is the recognition of this very need that has led to continuous changes in standards at the international level, of which our national discourse is a part.

Influence of International Standards

The impact of international standards has always been visible in the development of juvenile justice in India. The enactment of juvenile justice-related laws in this country, as we have seen, is itself a part of the colonial legacy, with the British rulers introducing measures similar to those being enacted in the United Kingdom.

Post-Independence, in 1960, following the second United Nations Congress on the Prevention of Crime and Treatment of Offenders in London, the Children Act, 1960 was passed to cater to the needs of the Union Territories.[15] To remove some inherent lacunae in that Act, the Children (Amendment) Act was passed in 1978.[16] The definition of 'child', however, still differed for boys and girls. As we have seen above, for boys it meant a person who had not attained the age of 16 years and for girls it was a person who was not yet 18 years. It was presented as a model act and was followed by the enactment of Children Acts in various other States that didn't already have them, after 1960.[17]

The Children Act, 1960 introduced four unique features. It provided for the constitution of two separate competent authorities, namely, a Children's Court to deal with delinquent children and a Child Welfare Board for neglected children. It prohibited the imposition of the death penalty or sentencing children to terms of imprisonment or keeping them in police stations under any circumstances, including for failure to pay fines or failure to find sureties and even during pendency of proceedings. It also created three categories of institutions for providing residential care to children—the Observation Home, the Juvenile Home and the Special Home.

In 1986, in conformity with the UN Standard Minimum Rules for the Administration of Juvenile Justice (more commonly referred to as the Beijing Rules),[18] the first national legislation on juvenile justice was enacted—the Juvenile Justice Act, 1986. The Beijing Rules, adopted on 29 November 1985, had in fact set the standard for the whole world to emulate. Clause 4.1 of the Rules reads as follows:

> In those legal systems recognizing the concept of the age of criminal responsibility for juveniles, the beginning of that age shall not be fixed at too low an age level, bearing in mind the facts of emotional, mental and intellectual maturity.

The Rules did not fix any specified age and left it to each country to frame their domestic laws, keeping in view the various relevant doctrines they may adhere to. The JJ Act,

1986 continued with the same definitions as in the Children Act for defining a 'child'—16 years for boys and 18 for girls. Continuing to embrace the welfarist approach, it addressed both 'delinquent' and 'neglected' children. This law used the term 'delinquent juvenile' (Section 2[e]) for a child who was found to have committed an offence and 'neglected juvenile' for a child who needed care and protection and included a whole range of vulnerable children (Section 2[l] i–v). And two parallel facilities were created for the two categories of children, as we have noted previously.

The introduction of the word 'juvenile' in place of 'child' itself was an impact of the adoption of international standards. (The current law has reverted to the use of the word child again.) Explaining the use of the term juvenile as against children in the previous law, the JJ Act, 1986, in Chapter 1 (Preliminary 1.1), explains that

> Though the subject matter and the provisions of the JJA are similar to those of the Children Act, 1960, the term 'juvenile justice'[19] had been substituted for 'children' in the title of the Act. This change may perhaps be attributed to the fact that 'juvenile justice' is currently being used in the United Nations. The Children Act, 1960 was preceded by the United Nations Declaration of the Rights of the Child in 1959. The JJA has been enacted a year after the Beijing Rules using the term juvenile justice were adopted by the General Assembly in 1985. Though the term 'juvenile justice' before the onset of delinquency may refer to social justice, after the onset of delinquency, it refers to justice in its normal juridical sense. The JJA provides for justice after the onset of delinquency. The Children Act, 1960 sought to do the same. The two Acts differ significantly in their territorial jurisdiction but that is not because of the difference between their titles. Therefore, the change

in the title brings about no material difference, in the 'juvenile justice' provided by the Children Act, 1960 or that under the JJA.[20]

General Comment No. 10, 2007 ('Children's Rights in Juvenile Justice', CRC/C/GC/10, 25 April 2007) to the UNCRC mentioned earlier, formulated by the Committee on the Rights of the Child reiterates why and how states must address offences by children separately from adults. General Comment No. 10 explains that children differ from adults in their physical and psychological development, and their emotional and educational needs and why such differences constitute the basis for the lesser culpability of children in conflict with the law. These and other differences are the reasons for a separate juvenile justice system and require different treatment for children. The protection of the best interests of the child means, for instance, that the traditional objectives of criminal justice, such as repression/retribution, must give way to rehabilitation and restorative justice objectives in dealing with child offenders. Of course, this has to be done in concert with attention to effective public safety.

Bearing in mind the standards prescribed in the UNCRC (which India ratified in 1992), the 1985 Beijing Rules, the United Nations Rules for the Protection of Juveniles Deprived of their Liberty (1990), and all other relevant international instruments, the Juvenile Justice (Care and Protection of Children) Act was enacted in India in the year 2000, and has been amended several times since.

Bringing our legislation into harmony with the UNCRC, this law defined juvenile simply as a person who has not completed 18 years. While still referring to the child who has committed an offence as *juvenile*, the JJ Act, 2000 used the term *child* to mean a 'child in need of care and protection (CNCP)' and laid out a list of children who fell into this category (Section 2[d]). Following precedent, the reason for including CNCP continued to be the fact these were children who were living on the edge and vulnerable to coming into conflict with the law for lack of timely intervention. Over the years, amendments to the law have gone to the extent of treating CICL found involved in petty offences and with an unfit family or no family as CNCP, thus transferring the matter from the Juvenile Justice Board to the Child Welfare Committee. This ensures that such children are not kept with those involved in heinous offences and are taken care of by the state till they complete 18 years of age.

What was particularly significant in the version of the JJ Act, as it was amended in 2015, was the inclusion of sixteen 'General Principles of Care and Protection of Children' (Section 3 [i–xvi]) that are meant to guide all actions taken to implement the law. I have always felt that the beauty of the JJ Act lies in this. Indeed, they form the soul of the statute. Of course they draw a lot from international standards and instruments. But they also reflect the spirit of the Constitution of India. They reflect the spirit and philosophy that underpins the law. Salient to my mind among these principles are the principle of presumption of innocence—all children must be presumed to be innocent of any mala fide or criminal intent up to the age of 18 years; the principle of dignity and worth—that all shall be treated with equal dignity and rights; the principle of diversion—unless absolutely necessary, the CICL must be dealt with without resorting to the criminal justice system; and the principle of fresh start—that except in special circumstances, all past records of any child in the juvenile justice system should be erased.

In Section 3(x) of the Act is enshrined the principle of equality and non-discrimination. Article 2 of the UNCRC insists on 'appropriate measures to ensure that the child is protected against all forms of discrimination or punishment on the basis of the status, activities, expressed opinions, or beliefs of the child's parents, legal guardians, or family members'. In its General Comment No. 10 mentioned above, the UN Committee on the Rights of the Child stated the need for taking 'necessary measures to ensure that all children… are treated equally [with] particular attention to de facto discrimination and disparities' that affect 'vulnerable groups of children, such as street children, children belonging to racial, ethnic, religious or linguistic minorities, indigenous children, girl children, children with disabilities and children who are repeatedly in conflict with the law (recidivists)'.

In 2019, the UN Committee on the Rights of the Child adopted General Comment No. 24 (2019) on Children's Rights in Juvenile Justice (CRC/C/GC/24) which replaced General Comment No. 10.[21] In adopting this General Comment, the Committee says:

> The Committee acknowledges that the preservation of public safety is a legitimate aim of the justice system, including the juvenile justice system. However, in the Committee's view this aim is best served by full respect for and implementation of the principles of juvenile justice as enshrined in the Convention on the Rights of the Child. The present general comment replaces the original general comment No. 10 (2007), and preserves the same spirit and philosophy.

It reiterates the need for treating children without discrimination (Paras 8 and 9).

The Beijing Rules too had emphasized that all children must be treated equally and that the standard minimum rules listed therein should be 'applied to juvenile offenders impartially, without distinction of any kind, for example as to race, colour, sex, language, religion, political or other opinions, national or social origin, property, birth or other status' (Rule 2.1).

This idea of equality and non-discrimination is closely tied to the idea that all children have the right to participate in decisions that concern them, and they must be given the opportunity to be heard. And it is explicitly included in the 2015 Act in Section 3(iii)—the principle of participation. It entails providing the children with an environment where they feel free to express themselves without fear of censure and the assurance that their opinions will be given due consideration in arriving at a decision. The right to be heard in administrative and judicial proceedings is one of the fundamental principles of juvenile jurisprudence, included in the UNCRC, the Beijing Rules, and the General Comment No. 10 of the UN Committee on the Rights of the Child. Article 12(2) of the UNCRC, for example, requires that a child be provided with the opportunity to be heard in any judicial or administrative proceedings affecting the child, either directly or through a representative or an appropriate body in a manner consistent with the procedural rules of national law.

One of the cardinal principles that the Act lays out is the principle of best interest—as explained in Section 3(xiii) of the JJ Act, 2015. It requires that all decisions regarding the child shall be based on the primary consideration that they are in the best interest of the child and are made to help the child realize his/her full potential. It follows that any decision taken regarding the child must ensure fulfilment of his/her basic rights and needs, identity, social well-being and physical, emotional and intellectual development.

An explanation of the best interest principle can be found in Article 3 of the UNCRC—and it is further clarified in General Comment No. 10 and General Comment No. 24—which argues for:

a) primary consideration to the child's best interests in all actions concerning children, whether undertaken by public or private social welfare institutions, courts of law, administrative authorities or legislative bodies;

b) taking appropriate legislative and administrative measures to ensure the well-being of children by providing necessary protection and care;

c) ensuring compliance of institutions, services and facilities responsible for the care or protection of children with the standards established by competent authorities, particularly in the areas of safety, health, in the number and suitability of their staff, as well as competent supervision.

Another key guiding idea included is the principle of family responsibility (Section 3[v]). It recognizes that the primary responsibility of care, nurture and protection of the child must be that of the biological family or adoptive or foster parents, which in and of itself must be considered a big step forward. With it are also included the principle of safety, to protect the child from harm, abuse or maltreatment while in contact with the system, or even after; the principle of the use of non-stigmatizing semantics, which shows a deep awareness of the harmful impact of 'adversarial or accusatory words' used against a child in custody; the principle of non-waiver of rights, which protects a child from losing any of his/her fundamental rights; and tied closely to the principle of fresh start mentioned above, the law crucially includes the principle of privacy and confidentiality, as well as the principle of repatriation and restoration to the family at the earliest after assessing the child's best interest.

If one were to try and sum up the approach the JJ Act, 2015 argues for, to ask what is fundamental to its philosophy of juvenile justice, so to speak, one need look no further than the principle of institutionalization as the last resort (Section 3[xii]). This is a direct echo of the Beijing Rules of 1985, Rule 17.1(c) of which says that 'deprivation of personal liberty shall not be imposed unless the juvenile is adjudicated of a serious act involving violence against another person or of persistence in committing other serious offences'. It follows Rule 17.1(b), which says that 'restrictions on the personal liberty of the juvenile shall be imposed only after careful consideration and shall be limited to the *possible minimum*' (emphasis added).

As should be evident from the discussion above, the juvenile justice law and the system it lays out, was designed from the very inception to address both prevention of crime by including both children who are vulnerable and hence likely to come in conflict with the law, and also children who fall through the safety net and end up committing an offence. It was designed to ensure that children are able to integrate into the mainstream of society. While our understanding of what justice for children constitutes has evolved over time, it can be safely asserted that at the heart of all legislation—including the Children Acts, the Act of 1986, as well as those of 2000 and 2015—is the best interest of the child. Unfortunately, as we shall see in the next chapter, it is a promise that is only too often undermined by the system itself.

3

THE STUMBLING BLOCKS

Child or Adult?: Politics and Societal Pressure

We have seen how the Juvenile Justice (Care and Protection of Children) Act, 2015 substantially expanded the scope of care and protection of children with specific reference to development, social reintegration and the adoption of a child-friendly approach, beyond what was there even in the legislation enacted in 2000. It recognizes the need for basic principles that need to guide the administration of juvenile justice in India as it continues to draw upon international texts and conventions.

It is significant that it has dropped the differential use of the terms 'juvenile' and 'child' for different categories of children and only uses the term child to describe all persons covered under the JJ Act, setting the age at 18 years.

But what is additional, and contentious, is the classification of offences committed by children into three categories—petty, serious and heinous. As has been mentioned earlier, the enactment of the JJ Act, 2015 was not entirely part of the natural progression of legal reform. It was in response to the huge outcry over the rape of a woman in 2012, in which a child aged 17 years and 10 months was involved, that the government of India gave in to public pressure to amend the law. While the cases against the adult accused were transferred to a fast-track court, the child was sent to the Juvenile Justice Board (JJB) to be dealt with according to the provisions of the JJ Act, 2000.

Triggered by reports from the press based on unconfirmed statements leaked to it, a public outrage had been generated against the juvenile implicated in the Nirbhaya case, and all such children by extension. The child accused was demonized by the media as being the most brutal, even though the same media later reported that this was not the case.[1] The board's order made it clear that in their testimonies neither Nirbhaya nor her male friend singled out the juvenile as the person who had brutally assaulted her with a rod resulting in an injury that eventually led to her death.[2] Even the Principal Magistrate looking at the case at the time said that the way our criminal justice system functions—even though there was not much direct evidence against him, by virtue of his presence at the scene of the commission of the crime—his conviction was a given. The problem was ensuring his safety, how he could be 'debranded [sic], so to say', and his rehabilitation in society, for which there was very little assistance that was forthcoming.

But by then the harm was done. As Professor Ved Kumari, now vice chancellor of the National Law University Odisha, says, 'There is a difference between democracy and "mobocracy". This is what the mobocracy wanted. The legislation gave in to that mobocracy, not democracy.' She further asks: 'Where were the voices of these children in this whole conversation? The Ministry dealing with both child and woman was only thinking about the safety of women.

But what about children? There was a conflict of interest in that very situation… [I]t is completely hypocritical to say the amendments are made keeping in mind the benefit of the child. What is being done for the children? Nothing.'[3] The floodgates, though, have already been opened. Why 16 and not lower is the question being asked.[4]

That 'children mature much faster these days' is something one gets to hear very often in conversations. But do they 'mature' faster? It is true that there is an earlier onset of puberty, not just in India,[5] but globally as well. Children certainly have access to more information because of access to the internet and social media. But are they really capable of processing the information? Who, if anyone, is actually helping them do so?

At a training session in April 2022 at the Judicial Academy of Odisha, renowned psychiatrist Dr Harish Shetty asked members of the audience, which consisted of Principal Magistrates of various JJBs and other key stakeholders from four states—Odisha, West Bengal, Chhattisgarh and Jharkhand—'How many of you believe that the age of the definition of CICL should be 16 years?' Almost half of the hands went up. And these were individuals in charge of implementing the law! They clearly did not believe in it, at least as it stood in the statute books. That is the power of what Prof Ved Kumari referred to as the 'mobocracy'.

One often finds, in conversations with people, that they confuse two very important concepts—minimum age of criminal responsibility (MACR) and age of juvenility. MACR is related to the concept of *doli incapax*—a legal maxim that assumes children to be incapable of harbouring criminal intent before a certain age and therefore incapable of recognizing the consequence of their actions. It thus follows that their actions are not to be construed as offences despite any resultant harm or injury. The MACR differs from country to country. In India it is 7 years. In Scotland it was raised from 8 to 12 in June 2019, but in England, Wales and Northern Ireland it remains 10 years. In the Netherlands and Canada, it is 12 years. Sweden, Finland and Norway have all set the MACR at 15 years. In the United States the age varies between States, set as low as 6 years in South Carolina and 7 years in thirty-five other states. Eleven years is the minimum age for federal crimes.[6]

The age of juvenility on the other hand refers to the age up to which the young offender will be treated as a child and *diverted into* the juvenile justice system. In India this is 18 years today. This is in keeping with international standards.

In arguments that we put forth against the lowering of the age of juvenility and of sending them into the adult system, preceding the amendment of the law in 2015, we had relied heavily on the writings of Lawrence Steinberg and Elizabeth Scott among others who have studied how the development of the brain influences behaviour.

In August 2018, I was taking my seat at a meeting—Cross-National Strategies to Advance Systems of Youth Justice and Child Protection—at the University of Leiden to find that the nameplate next to mine said Dr Lawrence Steinberg. Further down was Dr Elizabeth Scott! They were surprised to learn how much they had been quoted in our petitions on juvenile justice following the proposal for amending the law. That is because, sadly, we did not have any equivalent studies on brain science that analyse brain development and the behaviour of adolescents in the Indian context. Recognizing the gap in research that exists in the area of developmental psychology and child offending, Kalpana Purushothaman, who has also contributed to this book, undertook doctoral research on the subject of 'Mental Health Status and Counselling of Children in Conflict with the Law'. Of course, the law had by then already been amended and we couldn't use her findings.

Steinberg has written about how courts' decisions in the USA are increasingly influenced by findings from studies of brain development, and how they reflect the position that 'adolescents are less mature than adults in ways that mitigate their criminal culpability, and that adolescents' diminished blameworthiness makes it inappropriate to sentence them in ways that are reserved for individuals who are deemed fully responsible for their criminal acts'.[7]

Scott and Steinberg[8] explain that heightened risk-taking during adolescence is understood to be the result of a developmental asynchrony wherein inclinations to pursue exciting, potentially rewarding experiences are especially strong, but the ability to control such urges is still relatively immature. The tendency towards heightened sensation seeking is sparked by the hormonal changes of puberty, which are believed to increase activity in the brain's reward pathways, making individuals more attentive, sensitive and responsive to actual and potential rewards. This behaviour continues into the early twenties. They describe this period in a young person's life as a time when the 'accelerator' is pressed to the floor, but a good 'braking system' is not yet in place. Scott and Steinberg argue that it is this possibility—that the risky behaviour by adolescents and young adults, including their involvement in criminal activity, is a product of their psychological and social immaturity—that raises the question of whether the presumption of reduced culpability and greater potential for reform should be applied to young adult offenders as well as juveniles.[9]

Recognizing the importance of brain development, General Comment No. 24 (Para 22) to the UN Convention on the Rights of the Child states:

> Documented evidence in the fields of child development and neuroscience indicates that maturity and the capacity for abstract reasoning is still evolving in children aged 12 to 13 years due to the fact that their frontal cortex is still developing. Therefore, they are unlikely to understand the impact of their actions or to comprehend criminal proceedings. They are also affected by their entry into adolescence.

Even in its General Comment No. 20 (2016) on the Implementation of the Rights of the Child during Adolescence,[10] the Committee on the Rights of the Child noted that adolescence is a unique defining stage of human development characterized by rapid brain development, and this affects risk-taking, certain kinds of decision-making and the ability to control impulses.

In General Comment No. 24, the Committee encourages the governments of all countries:

> [To take] note of recent scientific findings, and to increase their minimum age accordingly, to at least 14 years of age. Moreover, the developmental and neuroscience evidence indicates that adolescent brains continue to mature even beyond the teenage years, affecting certain kinds of decision-making. Therefore, the Committee commends States parties that have a higher minimum age, for instance 15 or 16 years of age, and urges States parties not to reduce the minimum age of criminal responsibility under any circumstances, in accordance with article 41 of the Convention.[11]

Unfortunately, the Indian parliament came under political and public pressure created by one case of a barbaric gang rape in which one of the accused happened to be a child on the verge of attaining majority.[12] So, whatever gains had been made over the years through disciplines like criminology, penology, victimology, neuroscience and restorative justice, leading to the development of a progressive and forward-looking juvenile justice law, were ignored in the course of the formulation of a new law.[13]

In response to this 'public demand', the government introduced a provision for transfer of children committing 'heinous' crimes into the adult system after an assessment to determine if the offence was committed in an *adult frame of mind*. The only concession is that such children will not be sentenced to death or to life imprisonment without the possibility of release, and till they cross 18 years of age, will not be placed in adult prisons.

SECTION 15

(Preliminary assessment into heinous offences by Board)

1. In case of a heinous offence alleged to have been committed by a child, who has completed or is above the age of sixteen years, the Board shall conduct a preliminary assessment with regard to his mental and physical capacity to commit such offence, ability to understand the consequences of the offence and the circumstances in which he allegedly committed the offence, and may pass an order in accordance with the provisions of subsection (3) of section 18:

> Provided that for such an assessment, the Board may take the assistance of experienced psychologists or psycho-social workers or other experts.
>
> *Explanation*: For the purposes of this section, it is clarified that preliminary assessment is not a trial, but is to assess the capacity of such child to commit and understand the consequences of the alleged offence.

This provision for transfer into the adult criminal justice system was included in the law despite, on two separate occasions, the Supreme Court of India having upheld the constitutionality of the cut-off age of 18 years in the Juvenile Justice Act, and the need for a separate juvenile justice system for juvenile offenders irrespective of the nature of offence—*Salil Bali vs Union of India* (WP[C] No. 10 of 2013), and then again in *Dr Subramanian Swamy and Ors vs Raju and Anr* (Criminal Appeal No. 695 of 2014).

This provision remains one of the most contentious aspects of the law and has come in for severe criticism. According to Prof Ved Kumari, this provision is against the best interest of children, which as we have seen in the previous chapter is one of the key principles the law is guided by. She says the validity of this provision will have to be tested on the touchstone of Article 14 (which ensures equality and equal protection before law) and Article 15 (allowing the state to make special provision for children and women) of the Constitution of India. The government has chosen to define the child as an individual of up to the age of 18 years and in doing so has accepted classification into the categories of child and adult. Hence, according to Prof Ved Kumari, the sub-classification within it fails the test of 'reasonable' classification. This is because, given the objective of the JJ Act, any such sub-classification *must be only in favour of children*. Any punishment for children for commission of heinous offences or treating them as adults in certain circumstances is not part of the objective of this Act, which is to provide for care, protection, development, treatment and social reintegration of the children. According to her, it is also in contravention of India's obligations under the UNCRC.[14]

We would do well to keep Prof Ved Kumari's warning in mind: 'The actual arbitrariness that will result in the cases of transfer of children and the consequent orders that will be passed by the Children's Courts without any guidance are something to be witnessed in the times to come. The arbitrariness will be further exacerbated in the absence of any scientific methods by which psychiatrists and psychologists *may* assess whether the offence was committed with a child-like or adult-like mind.'[15] (Emphasis added)

The UN Committee on the Rights of the Child too has recognized that leaving the determination of capacity or maturity of a child to commit an offence to the judicial officers can lead to discriminatory practices. To quote from the Committee's General Comment No. 24 (Para 43):

> The assessment of this maturity is often left to the court/judge, sometimes without the requirement of involving a psychological expert (who are often not available in developing states), and results in practice in the use of the lower minimum age in cases of serious crimes. The system of two minimum ages is often not only confusing, but leaves much to the discretion of the court/judge and may result in discriminatory practices.

The Committee had previously, in General Comment No. 10 (Para 34) already 'express[ed] its concern about the practice of allowing exceptions to a MACR which permit the use of a lower minimum age of criminal responsibility in cases where the child, for example, is accused of committing a serious offence or where the child is considered mature enough to be held criminally responsible. The Committee strongly recommends that States parties set a MACR that does not allow, by way of exception, the use of a lower age'.

To avoid such arbitrary practices, the Committee recommends in General Comment No. 24 (Para 30):

> [T]hose States parties that limit the applicability of their child justice system to children under the age of 16 years (or lower), or that allow by way of exception that certain children are treated as adult offenders (for example, because of the offence category), change their laws to ensure a non-discriminatory full application of their child justice system to all persons below the age of 18 years at the time of the offence.

How is the law implemented? Stories from across the country differ so greatly, and the quality of justice is so disparate that it's impossible to capture every detail. It does not help in the least that the JJ Act, 2015 has 112 sections—not all of which are clear and cogent.

Psychologists say that there is no way to determine mental capacity (or 'adult frame of mind' as it has come to be colloquially referred to). Besides, given that India has over 700 districts, and each district has a JJB, there are not enough trained psychologists who can assist the JJBs to undertake such assessments. In their absence, it is mostly the Principal Magistrates who decide on the assessment. As judicial officers, they feel superior to the social worker members, who themselves are prone to be intimidated by the magistrate. This can lead to some peculiar assumptions and methods applied.

For example, at a meeting in which I was present, a young Principal Magistrate, on being asked how he decides that a child who has been produced before him should be treated as an adult (under Section 15), replied, 'I give him a situation. I tell him, suppose you were walking with your sister and someone misbehaved, what would you do? Based on his reaction I decide if he is to be treated as an adult or not. If he chooses violence, then clearly he knows the consequences of his action and is showing maturity.'

Another magistrate posted in a predominantly tribal district, nowhere close to an airport, said, 'When an airplane flies in the sky, I ask them: Is that a bird or an aeroplane? Based on the answer, I decide.'

Perhaps these examples seem almost extreme. I would have thought so too, had I not heard them myself.

There are of course also those who, once posted as Principal Magistrates, recognize the importance of their position—how they can make a change in the lives of children. And they go out of their way to do so. That is why Arul Verma, a former Principal Magistrate in a JJB in Delhi, says, 'The amendment to the law may not be to our liking and may even prick the conscience of many. But as adjudicators, and as adherents of law we have to interpret it in the best way possible, all the while ensuring that the rights of children are protected.'[16] While there are others like him, there are many more who see being in the JJB as a punishment posting. They care little for the children presented before them and make no effort to uphold the spirit of the law, even though they may be implementing it as per the letter of the law.

Although there is not enough data collected on the transfer provision, anecdotal evidence gathered shows that most JJBs find it easier to simply transfer 16–18-year-olds who have committed serious offences into the adult system.[17] Life imprisonments are already being ordered.[18] In June 2019, an Andhra Pradesh court awarded life imprisonment to a young offender (he is now above 18 years but had committed the offence when he was less).[19] There are similar reports from other states as well.[20]

It took an appeal to the High Court of Bombay to set aside the order directing that a 17-year-old booked for the murder of his 3-year-old neighbour in Mumbai be tried as an adult. Both the Mumbai city JJB as well as a Children's Court had directed that he be tried as an adult under the JJ Act, 2015. Setting aside these orders, the Bombay High Court directed that the accused be tried as a minor, saying the Act is reformative and not retributive. The Bombay High Court observed: '[Trial as an adult] is not a default choice; [but] a conscious, calibrated one. And for that, all the statutory criteria must be fulfilled.'[21]

In his order the judge said that while the JJB had relied on these two reports—the social investigation report prepared by the probation officer, dated 18.08.2018, and the mental health report from three mental health experts of the JJ Group of Hospitals, dated 10.04.2017—it had undertaken no independent assessment, and that if the Board's criteria of evaluation were followed, 'then every case becomes an open-and-shut case'. According to the High Court, just because the statute permits a child of 16 years and above to stand trial as an adult in case of heinous offences, it did not mean that all those children should be subjected to adult punishment. One of the key observations the court made was the following:

> [E]ssentially, the trial in the regular court is offence-oriented; in the juvenile court, it is offender-oriented. In other words, in the children's court, societal safety and the child's future are balanced. For an adult offender, prison is the default opinion; for a juvenile it is the last resort… [D]espite the amendment only a miniscule number of cases are actually being sent to adult courts, which is reflective of a sensitive and vigilant judiciary.[22]

Reassuring as this final observation is, there are several procedural issues as well that are far from ideal in the JJ Act, such as the time frame of three months within which the need to transfer the child into the adult system must be determined. This timeline poses serious questions not just about the legality of this process but also its practicality. According to Prof Ved Kumari, 'This time frame does not require that the assessment should be done after the police files its final report in the case confirming prima facie a case of heinous offence has been made against the child. In the absence of a final report, any assessment on the ability of the child to have committed the offence with a childlike frame of mind or not proceeds on the assumption that the child had indeed committed the offence on the basis of the complaint received.'[23] This kind of process and the resultant stigma for the child goes against the very principles of the JJ Act.

Examination of orders passed by the various High Courts, based on appeals regarding preliminary assessments, show time and again their orders indicating how the JJBs as well as Children's Courts across the country are not applying their mind. For example, in the Bombay High Court case discussed earlier, the order says, 'The JJ Board has undertaken no independent assessment; it has, in fact, heavily relied on the Social Investigation Report and MH [Mental Health] Report.

So its opinion, in the strict sense, cannot be branded an "expert opinion". The same reasoning applies to the appellate order, too. That said, the two reports the Board has relied on are, indeed, expert opinions: one rendered by a Probation Officer and the other by a panel of doctors. But neither report brings out into open any exceptional circumstances that compel the older juvenile to face the trial as an adult.'[24] Clearly, while Section 16 of the JJ Act uses the term '*may*' with respect to seeking the support of experts, the High Court shows an inclination to interpret it as '*shall*', underscoring the necessity of such support, but more importantly, it goes further to demand a more proactive role of the Board in dealing with these children.

There are other contentious issues as well that emerge from the orders. For example, in an appeal against a preliminary assessment order passed by a JJB, one High Court wondered whether it was trying to determine the capacity/maturity of the child to *commit the offence*,[25] while in another appeal a different High Court asked whether the purpose of a preliminary assessment was to determine the capacity/maturity of the child to *withstand an adult trial process*.[26]

Or consider, for example, the case of Durga Meena—a 17-year-old girl who suffered a violent marriage and killed her husband—who was charged for murder and subjected to a preliminary assessment. No assistance from any mental health experts was taken and a copy of the assessment report was not given to the child. Eventually, she was tried as an adult and convicted. On appeal to the High Court, the order noted that no assistance of a psychologist with expertise in working with children in difficult circumstances was sought in the proceedings and that the child was sent and admitted in the psychiatry department of a hospital based on some random secret report (a copy whereof was not provided to her). The court also noted that the Principal Magistrate had failed to take into account the circumstances in which the child was driven to commit the offence because of the conduct of the victim. It concluded that the appellant did not murder her husband in furtherance of any preconceived design or in a cold, calculated manner and that the Board's order was passed in an absolutely mechanical and laconic manner, there thus being no justification for her trial as an adult.[27]

While these are observations of the High Courts, conversations with practitioners across States confirm how often officials in charge are inclined to send the children in the 16–18-year age group, if apprehended for serious offences, into the adult system. That indeed has become the default option instead of the option of last resort. In fact, an examination of some of the preliminary assessments conducted using certain prescribed formats developed by JJBs or State governments show the inadequacy of these assessments as well as the arbitrariness with which recommendations are made.

In the absence of a proper birth certificate, which remains a gap in India, and the fact that there may be many children who do not attend school, and hence may not be able to provide a school certificate (something that the law asks for), age verification remains a contentious issue to begin with.

Recognizing the arbitrariness of this provision of assessment of maturity leading to transfer to the adult system, Additional Sessions Judge of the Dwarka District Courts, Vishal Gogne, introduced the concept of a 'neo-adult' in his order in a bail matter concerning a 19-year-old who had been arrested for murder.[28]

Judge Gogne argued that while the juvenile justice dispensation did undergo a significant change in the aftermath of the Nirbhaya case, rendering children accused of heinous offences in the age group of 16 to 18 years also liable to be tried as adults in suitable cases, '*the inconstancy of the law related to juveniles in India is not matched by any inconsistency in the principles governing bail*'. He further stated that multiple decisions of the Hon'ble Apex Court and High Courts have favoured release of young offenders on bail pending trial in order that the apparently regressive influences of the jail environment be avoided.

But what was even more significant was that the concept of the neo-adult that he introduced was applied to determine why a 19-year-old shall be treated as a young person who needs special treatment. In his judgement, Judge Gogne says:

> The applicant, 19 years in age, is not quite a child in the eye of the law but is yet only a neo adult. This court would propose that if a child (between the age 16 to 18 years) can be treated as an adult for the purpose of trial in heinous offences, a child who has just about crossed the legislated age of adulthood i.e. 18 years and remains a young adult (19–20 years) can certainly be afforded the protection of his liberty akin to a child in conflict with law... Such young alleged offenders may therefore be released on bail not only honoring [*sic*] the principle of presumption of innocence but also in recognition of the principle of 'best interest' which may again be extrapolated to neo adults from the Juvenile Justice regime. If admitted to bail, the applicant, a student, may yet gainfully pursue his best interest till trial adjudicates upon his culpability.

Because of the attitude of the lawmakers as well as the general public towards children who offend, the first course of action is to treat them as adults and send them to adult prison. This was in practice even before the 2015 law came into force.

On 11 May 2012, the Delhi High Court had passed a thirty-three-page judgement addressing the issue of incarcerating juveniles in jails meant for adult offenders. Underlining that this was against the law, the court laid down exhaustive directions for every agency of the criminal justice system—police, magistrates, prisons, and legal-aid authorities—to protect juveniles from the 'hardship of the adult penal system'.[29] Explaining the gravity of the situation, the judgement said:

> It is pointed out that many times when the accused persons are arrested by the Police and even when they happen to be children, they are lodged in Tihar Jail and subjected to the hardship of Adult Criminal Justice System. This may happen due to sheer negligence, omission or even deliberately. In support of this plea, it is mentioned that under Right to Information Act, 2005, information was received by the applicant from Central Jail No. 7 which discloses that during the period October, 2010 to August, 2011, 114 persons were shifted from Tihar Jail to Observation Homes after they were found to be juveniles. It is thus stated that without proper care being taken by the Police Authorities at the time of arrest to find out whether the concerned person is a juvenile or adult, they are lodged in the jails. It is further mentioned that generally from appearance of the persons arrested, it can be made out that he is a child. But in many cases in spite of the family of the persons arrested producing the birth certificate etc. to show that the person arrested is a child, still these evidences are ignored by the police and only when enquiry is conducted determining the age and it is ultimately found that the accused person is a child, is

he shifted to Observation Homes. In the process, such
children are subjected to the hardship of Adult Criminal
Justice System in the first instance which would have been
easily avoided if proper care is taken at the time of arrest
of such persons.

However, in August 2021, *The Quint* reported that even
after over two decades of the enactment of the JJ Act, 2000,
incarceration of juveniles in 'adult jails' remains a bleak
reality. In a reply to an RTI application filed on 8 August
2020 to all the sixteen jails of the Tihar prison complex, it was
revealed that at least 123 prisoners were declared juveniles
in 2019–20. This figure was, however, obtained from just
eight jails in Tihar.[30] There was no reply from the remaining
eight. Interestingly, of the eight jails that did reply to the
RTI application, five mentioned that they do not maintain
any data on the identification and declaration of prisoners as
juveniles, thereby violating the obligations set by the Delhi
High Court in its 2012 order.

Examining the various issues that lead to children
being sent to adult prisons, *The Quint* found that despite
the order of the High Court, often, arresting officers mark
the accused as an adult because of his inability to produce
proof of age, despite his physical appearance suggesting the
opposite. When in doubt, the police favoured declaring the
accused an adult. Sadly, even the magistrates seemed to skip
the assessment of the physical appearance of the accused.
Around 85 per cent of the prisoners who approached legal-
aid lawyers claiming juvenility claimed that they were not
represented by a lawyer when they were brought before the
magistrate. They complained about magistrates remanding
them to prison almost mechanically, based solely on the
paperwork submitted by the police.[31] There clearly appears to

be absolutely no application of the judicial mind—let alone heart and conscience.

The fact is that a majority of these children appearing before them are poor and often illiterate, with no knowledge of the law or their rights. They stated that arresting officers did not inform them about their rights under the Juvenile Justice Act, or of the fact that they had to produce proof of age. What is worse, the arresting officer, who is usually a *havaldar* (constable), is at times not well versed with the law himself, let alone sufficiently familiar with the provisions of the Juvenile Justice Act, nor adequately trained and sensitized on how to deal with children in conflict with the law.[32]

Some Challenges in Dealing with the System

The troubles for offending children, however, go beyond those that arise out of unsympathetic interpretations of the law or indifferent government officials. One of the biggest challenges that the juvenile justice system in India faces is the lack of resources—financial and human resources, as well as infrastructural. This has been the case in the past, and continues to be so. Several questions immediately arise given the state of affairs: Should children have to bear the brunt of lack of resources and the resultant failure of the proper implementation of the law? Is the reform system not working because the state has failed children, or is it because the children are 'un-reformable' and hence need harsher punishments?

Ratna Saxena, who was the superintendent of the Prayas Home for Boys in Delhi for many years, describes her predicament: 'Every new day brought new challenges! Some from the authorities, some from the staff who worked there and some from the children themselves who were sent to the Observation Home.'[33]

The challenges she faced were numerous. But the first and foremost was funds. In the absence of adequate financial resources everything else becomes still more challenging—approvals for any new projects/programmes to keep the children involved, staff salaries, providing nutritious food, or maintaining cleanliness. Indeed, it must have been maddening, but with patience and perseverance, she kept going.

Premoday Khakha, who has also spent time as a superintendent of an Observation Home in Delhi, says that in his experience, children being placed in protective custody has become the central purpose of the juvenile justice system. 'I often wonder why the fundamental principles describe the institution as a measure of last resort when almost every child apprehended for the alleged lawbreaking is pushed into the den. Many think that the institution is a refinery unit that magically reforms the nature and character of a person,' he says. According to him the principle of repatriation and restoration of a child to a family set-up cannot be substituted with a 'mechanized Individual Care Plan[34] in any institution'.[35]

A sitting member of a JJB[36] told me that his Board had about 2,500 pending cases. His is only one of the many in his State. And despite the lockdown-like situation for a long time during 2020 and 2021 it received at least two to four new cases every day. 'Every day we take up 50-plus [existing] cases. We have only two stenos. So making out routine orders takes till 5 pm. Then there are the new cases which require much more attention. Is it any surprise that we simply cannot give the kind of time and attention that each case deserves?

My board has been allotted three probation officers, but only two are with us in the Board. I am not sure why we never see the third who is posted with us on paper. We need Social Investigation Reports for bail as well as for making the Individual Care Plans as laid down in the law—all of which becomes impossible under the circumstances.'

Bipasha Roy, a former member of the JJB in Kolkata says that challenges come in various forms, from various people and from various corners. The foremost challenge, of course, lies in helping the child deal with the implications of the word 'juvenile'. As children enter the juvenile justice system and get hauled through it, the stigma of being offenders sticks to them. Beginning with the police station, through the Board to the child care institution (CCI),[37] and back to the community, the child is marked as an offender, whether explicitly or implicitly.[38] But there are other more mundane, though seemingly insurmountable, problems as well.

The officer in charge of a Children's Home and the police officer in charge of a particular case are ironically called 'Child Welfare Officer' (CWO) and 'Child Welfare Police Officer', respectively, in the JJ Act (Section 2 [17] and [18]). I recall how at a police training session, a policeman said sarcastically, '*Madam, hum to police ki naukri karne aaye the. Aap logon ne to is kanoon se humein social worker bana diya.*' (Madam, we had come to join the police force. Through this law you have turned us into social workers.)

It is not as if the police do not have to perform their regular policing tasks as well. That is what complicates matters. According to Bipasha Roy, the behaviour of the police towards the children would sometimes be directly proportional to the volume of law-and-order situations that they had to handle. She shares, 'If the CWO has been through a gruelling night shift, and when it's time for him to go home, at dawn, the case of a juvenile comes in, the CICL will have to face the brunt of the CWOs frustration. I remember the CWOs complaining to us in the Board about a lack of designated SJPUs[39]/CWOs and child-friendly spaces in the police station. This was often used as an excuse for losing patience with the CICL and keeping them in lock-up. Once I was told by police personnel that they put these CICL in lock-up in order to save them from public thrashings that they might have to suffer.'

As per the guidelines for police officers dealing with CICL, they cannot be in uniform when with children. This is encouraged to ensure the police appear 'child-friendly'. The practical issue is that when they are not with children, and are performing other policing duties, they have to be in uniform. They cannot suddenly run off and change into civil clothes when a case concerning a child comes up. And yet the JJB will indict them if they appear in uniform while accompanying a child. If they have to apprehend a child who has been caught with adults, what kind of clothes must the police be in? they ask. The investigating officer (IO) has to produce the adults in court in uniform and produce the CICL in the JJB in civil clothes—and this may happen in the course of the same day. Needless to say, the police complain and ridicule this provision. And frankly, I cannot blame them. Should the uniform not be turned into something children do not fear and indeed trust? Unfortunately, the mistrust is a product of the usual behaviour of the police with the children, which has become the norm over many decades, and it isn't easily overcome.

To mention another, among the many, peculiarities of the legal system, many magistrates and board members have shared with me how they are most conflicted when they have to deal with what have commonly come to be called 'love cases'. Having set the age of consent at 18 years, all sexual activity below this age is a criminal offence according to the POCSO Act, 2012. But the reality is that adolescents below the age of 18 years do have sexual contact and relationships. They even run away and marry—sometimes both parties are below 18 years and sometimes one party, usually the girl, is below 18 and her partner is an adult. But even if both are below 18 years, one becomes the offender (CICL) with a case registered against him while the girl becomes the victim who needs care and protection (CNCP).

Bipasha Roy recalls a 'victim', a girl shouting at her saying that she was happy that she had run away from home and would do so again if given a chance. The CICL (her boyfriend) who was produced by the police sat crying his heart out in the waiting area saying that had he known elopement would have such consequences, he would never have run away with her.

Transportation of children in conflict with the law is yet another challenge. The children are not allowed to be handcuffed. In the absence of vehicles, the police are sometimes forced to use public transport, and often over long distances and durations. The children in their charge are not always easy to manage or hold on to. If they run away, the police person in charge has to face dire consequences. This is in the districts. In the cities, most often the children are transported in the same caged vans that transport adult prisoners.

Bipasha Roy recalls, 'I was waiting in front of the JJB to receive the CICL who were being escorted by the police. As the black, caged police van (with Kolkata Police written in bold white letters on the sides) came to a halt in front of the building, a small crowd assembled and began talking about the "*bachcha ashamis*" (young criminals) getting out of the van. I cringe whenever I recollect the distressed countenance of the CICL who hung their head and walked in a file to the lift with their police escorts clutching their hands tightly. The next day, I visited the Lalbazar Kolkata Police headquarters to complain about this and request them to provide ordinary civil vehicles to escort the CICL. I was told that since there was a massive shortage of vehicles, this was not possible. They looked at me and said with a straight face that if the DWCD [Department of Women and Child Development] could provide the vehicles, they would decorate them with streamers and balloons and make them child-friendly for the CICL.' The sarcasm was not lost on Bipasha. But she was helpless.

I too have seen what a challenge it is for the alleged child offender to continue with his education given the stigma attached. They are often forced to change their school. Many a time, it is the parents of other students who threaten the principal with withdrawing their children if the concerned child continues to study in the school. This is a common refrain from all persons who work with CICL.

The aim of the JJ Act is to be able to reform. Every child needs a special and unique approach which depends on a proper and comprehensive Social Investigation Report (SIR), an Individual Care Plan (ICP) based on that report, and a follow-up by the probation officer (PO). In the absence of trained personnel to prepare a comprehensive SIR, what one is left with is an inadequate ICP and at best a lackadaisical follow-up of the order by the Board to monitor the re-integration of the child upon release. Experts are hardly consulted by the PO while drawing up the SIR and their recommendations do nothing to help frame the ICP. The JJ Act directs each dispositional order passed by the Board to be accompanied by an ICP which is to be drawn in consultation with the child and his parents/guardians. The entire purpose of the child being drawn into the juvenile justice system is defeated when children are re-integrated into society without any structured support from the stakeholders/caregivers for their rehabilitation. Of course, as was pointed out by the JJB member earlier, there simply are not enough probation officers to ensure that.

Throughout the time that I have been engaged with the juvenile justice system, we have seen that one of the prime movers for children ending up in the world of offending is in fact addiction and the need for money to buy the drugs. They either peddle drugs or commit other offences under its influence. However, there are hardly any deaddiction centres, commensurate with the number of children who are addicted, which offer treatment free of cost. Despite orders from JJBs, there are hidden costs at these centres which compel poor parents to withdraw their children. Moreover, without any hand-holding and follow-up, these children are inevitably sucked back into bad habits after their release from the rehab centres. It is an unfortunate reality that endures.

And in all this, I haven't yet touched on the issue of mental health, which compounds all other problems that a child care worker has to deal with, to say nothing of what the children have to suffer themselves. The reality is that the need for mental health services, if acknowledged, is never taken seriously or adequately addressed. To cite just one very minor issue, for example, the Delhi government has signed an MOU with an organization to provide mental health services. But they send very young students, mostly female, to assess and support the boys lodged in the Observation

Homes and Special Homes. It doesn't require much imagination to recognize why this is not just inadequate, it's also inappropriate. In our own experience at HAQ, we have found that male counsellors are more effective for older boys. Similar is the case with the government appointed counsellors and social workers. They are often young and inexperienced. Older and more experienced mental health experts are imperative if the children are to be helped at all.

Although there is a system of capacity building for CWC and JJB members, their sessions are held at specific times. The members are appointed depending upon vacancies, and most often they have to hit the ground running—with no orientation or training. They pretty much learn on the job, and attend the workshops as and when they happen. And I am sure that in the 700 districts of India, not even this minimal service we have in Delhi for juvenile offenders is available!

For all the shortcomings of the law, the legal system, the lack of training or empathy among the government personnel, however, the foremost challenge that the cause of juvenile justice faces remains an unsympathetic citizenry. Justice D.S. Naidu, delivering his judgement in a landmark case on juvenile justice, *Mohamed Huzaifa Javed Ahmed vs State of Maharashtra* in 2019, made a poignant observation about what is happening to children and what the offenders are made out to be:

> A universally accepted ideal is that children are dependent and deficient in mental and physical capacities, and are in need of Juvenile Justice Board guidance. Perhaps, initially, a multi-visual medium like TV; later, a globe devouring internet (appropriately, ominously worded as 'world wide

web'), and finally—and fatally—the post-truth social media have let the children, especially the adolescents, leapfrog into the adult world. Mostly it is a crash-landing, with disastrous consequences. So, the childhood innocence is the casualty. These devices may have made a child bypass his or her childhood, sadly. Then, naturally, the theory of reduced culpability for juveniles relative to adults has taken a statutory dent. The good-old-days icon of a truant child seems to get replaced by the modern-day mascot of a violent predator.[40]

Unlike the perception that many have, placing children in the juvenile justice system is not to let offending children 'walk free'. On the contrary, it is to ensure that children recognize and understand the consequences of their 'act', and are held accountable for it. It is only the system of accountability that is different. A note on the US government website youth.gov best describes what juvenile justice ought to be about: 'It operates according to the premise that children and young persons are fundamentally different from adults, both in terms of level of responsibility and potential for rehabilitation. The primary goals of the juvenile justice system, in addition to maintaining public safety, are skill development, habilitation, rehabilitation, addressing treatment needs, and successful reintegration of youth into the community'.[41]

It is important that societies give all children a second chance to make a fresh start. Is that not what we would do for our own children were they to lose their way and end up in the wrong place? Why should it be different for 'those' children? Just like adults, there will be those who may not reform, those that reoffend. But one wonders if that is reason enough to let the system for reforming juvenile offenders remain as it is, with all that it portends for their future and ours.

4

THE CHILDREN WHO 'OFFEND'

This case before us is on a letter dated November 28, 1980 addressed to the Court by one Dr Vasudha Dhagamwar, a researcher and Social Scientist working in the Santhal Parganas of the State of Bihar. It represents one more instance of the utter callousness and indifference of our legal and judicial system to the under-trial prisoners languishing in the jails. It seems that once a person accused of an offence is lodged in the jail everyone forgets about him and no one bothers to care what is happening to him. He becomes a mere ticket number—a forgotten specimen of humanity—cut off and alienated from the society, an unfortunate victim of a heartless legal and judicial system which consigns him to long unending years of oblivion in jail.

This is how the judgement, authored by Justice P.N. Bhagwati in *Kadra Pahadiya and Ors vs State of Bihar* on 17 December 1980, begins.

The story goes back to 1972. Four boys of the Pahadiya tribe belonging to the Santhal Parganas, Bihar, were arrested in connection with a murder case; two of them on 26 November and the other two on 19 December. They were around 8–14 years of age and, according to the jail wardens, apparently innocent. Their ages were put down as 18–24 years during the registration of the case. The boys were committed to the sessions court in July 1974 and the trial was posted for 30 August 1977. But the case was never heard. Eight years later, luck finally smiled on the Pahadiya boys, Kadra, Chamra, Jame and Jome. On a visit to the jail in the course of her research, civil rights and legal activist (late) Vasudha Dhagamwar chanced upon their case and wrote to the Supreme Court. Vasudha in her letter petitioning the Supreme Court of India had emphasized that they could not have been more than 9 to 11 years old when they were arrested, because on enquiry the jail staff told her that the petitioners were 'naked goat-herds' when they first came to jail. When she found them, they looked about 18 to 22 years old. And they had been in prison for over nine years already! The Supreme Court took her letter up as a public interest litigation. The case finally opened for hearing in January 1981. The boys were acquitted a month later, after their entire boyhood was lost in prison, where they had spent their days doing manual work for the staff. Annoyed with such callous neglect of the boys by the local police and magistrates, Dhagamwar decided to fight for compensation. In 1986, the Supreme Court awarded Rs 5,000 as interim compensation to each of the boys.

This was also the year when India's first Juvenile Justice Act was passed, which defined a juvenile (Section 2[h]) as 'a boy who has not attained the age of sixteen years or a girl who has not attained the age of eighteen years'. But the final orders—with respect to some matters in the case—for the four Pahadiya boys, who were definitely juveniles when they allegedly committed the offence as per the new law, had still not come till 2000, fourteen years later, the year the new JJ Act was enacted!

I had heard this story from Vasudha when I had joined MARG in 1986, and the hearings for the case were still going on. I never realized that this story would keep coming back to me as I would myself begin to navigate the juvenile justice system.

That young boys who are poor are the ones who are 'picked up' and also get lost in the system is nothing new. That's what had happened to Ramesh in 2005, whose case was discussed earlier. Had his mother not come to us, and had we not helped file a habeas corpus petition, he may have remained languishing in Tihar Jail as an undertrial. He may not have had a Vasudha Dhagamwar discovering him in jail either.

We have seen in the previous chapter how, despite the High Court order of 2012, children continue to languish in adult jails. *The Quint*'s interviews conducted with ten jail-visiting lawyers empanelled with the Delhi State Legal Services Authority (DALSA) revealed that the main reason children land up in adult prisons is because most of them, like Ramesh, come from socio-economically underprivileged groups, with little to no official documentation. While many of them are migrants from other States who have come to Delhi for work, there are others, who run away from home to escape broken or abusive families. These children do not have a permanent residence, often live on the streets or in unauthorized colonies and are therefore unable to provide proof of residence. Because they also lack education and are unable to present legitimate proof of age at the time of arrest, they are written off as adults. One of the legal-aid lawyers empanelled in the West District of Delhi interviewed by

The Quint, echoed the sentiments of these children when he asked, 'How can you expect a homeless boy to show Aadhaar? How do you expect an illiterate boy to show a school leaving certificate? That too as they are being arrested!'[1]

The 'juvenile offender' in the Nirbhaya case became the face of all 'juveniles' across the country and across all times. He was portrayed as a monster and the worst perpetrator by the police, who fed this to the media which further amplified it. Needless to say, the public wanted him hanged. Hence, even when the investigating officer, Mr Anil Sharma, put out a statement to the contrary, no one cared to listen—not the media, nor the public.[2] Misinformation about the law made members of the public, a significant number of them at the very least, actually come to believe that children who offend just walk free, that they feel no remorse and that they can never be reformed. They needed to be put away—away from public view. One television anchor even said, 'Imagine *that fellow* must be walking freely around you…and you will never know. How unsafe is that?'[3] Such is the level of prejudice and fear.

The philosophy behind the juvenile justice law and those who propagate it is clear. They do not condone the offences— some of which are gruesome and horrendous. All they believe in is allowing the young offender to get a second chance to reform and reintegrate into society. They recognize that this is no easy task. It requires faith and skill—faith in the innate good within the young offenders and their capacity to reform, and skill for providing the support services these young people need. But most importantly, they recognize socio-economic circumstances, mental health and related issues, the violence that children witness growing up, as contributing factors, for though these do not lessen the gravity of the offence they certainly mitigate the culpability of the child.

While one needs to keep in mind the age of the apprehended child—it is the older children who are more often to be found to be in contact with the law—it does not necessarily mean they are functioning with an 'adult frame of mind'. In fact, as was discussed before, evidence of significant changes in brain structure during childhood and adolescence strongly suggests that cognitive characteristics are associated with biological immaturity of the brain and an imbalance among developing brain systems.[4] This implies dual systems—one involved in cognitive and behavioural control and the other involved in socio-emotional processes. The part of the brain that influences pleasure-seeking, risk-taking behaviours and emotional reactivity, develops faster than or more rapidly than the part that supports self-control.[5]

It naturally follows that young people can also be more susceptible to triggers for offending such as poverty, substance abuse, mental illness and cognitive disability. Although many such issues afflict adult offenders too, they can cause greater problems for children because of their physical, mental and emotional immaturity. What is more, they can even be at higher risk of becoming addicted to alcohol and drugs because of peer pressure, in turn leading to a higher risk for offending.[6] This is a fact that I have personally observed in my interaction with young offenders. The number of children who were addicted to various substances was so high in Delhi, the Juvenile Justice Committee of the Delhi High Court even decided to set up a de-addiction centre for children in conflict with the law in the same compound as the Observation Home for Boys (OHB) in the Sewa Kutir Complex in Kingsway Camp in 2011.

Chirag,[7] who had been sent to one such OHB in Delhi, was one of the few boys one could say came from 'privileged circumstances' but ended up in the system. He had not yet committed any serious offence, but the Child Welfare Committee (CWC) feared that for lack of timely intervention he would, given that he was addicted to alcohol and drugs. The social worker dealing with Chirag reports this conversation between them when she was taking him to the Vidyasagar Institute of Mental Health and Neuro & Allied Sciences (VIMHANS) to consult a psychiatrist: 'I can't cancel the party, that will be very embarrassing for me,' said Chirag.

'And what do you do at these parties? Who pays for the parties?'

'Nothing much. We rent a farm house and party there. Our parents pay for the parties; one party costs about 60,000 rupees. About 100 children get invited.'

'What about the food? And do you all drink?'

'We get the food from Old Delhi—it's the best! And so cheap! And yes, we pop a bottle of champagne to kick off the party for show. We drink that, and Breezers and beers.'

'And you drive a car?'

'Yes, it's all right, nothing happens.'

'But do you know that it is illegal for you to drive before you are 18?'

A confused pause. And for a fraction of a second his expression betrays his words because he knows that he is in the wrong.

The social worker continues the conversation. She asks him, 'Your mother says you beat your parents and break things around the house if you don't get what you want. Is that true?'

'Yes, it happens... Things break... I don't like it that she is so pushy all the time,' Chirag answers nonchalantly, in a very calm voice.

But Chirag was not always like this. He was a high achiever in academics, and a budding professional cyclist two years ago. He is the only child of his parents, and they live with Chirag's father, Ayushman's parents and siblings, in a joint family. Ayushman contributes to his father's business and Shobha, his mother, is a housewife. Growing up, Chirag has witnessed violence between his parents. Ayushman is a recovering alcoholic, who also suffers from depression.

According to Shobha, Chirag's behaviour took a turn for the worse two years ago, when his father had a serious accident which was suspected to be attempted suicide. He was hospitalized for three months and Shobha couldn't pay adequate attention to Chirag during this span of time. She feels that it was around this time that his behaviour began to worsen. Shobha acknowledges that the atmosphere at home is one of the reasons for Chirag's predicament today. 'His grandmother interferes in a negative way; there is no cooperation at home and no unity in the joint family. The family also blames me for Ayushman's situation.' As a child, Chirag had always been very active and bright and a child one may describe as 'naughty'.

Chirag is only a prototype for many other children who are at the cusp of slipping into the downward spiral of becoming the 'demonized' children the media, the society and the state are up in arms against. If, like Chirag, they are not provided with the necessary support by the institutions that should care for them—the state, the family as well as society at large—they gradually fall deeper and deeper into crimes of a more serious nature. In Chirag's case, his mother, who was his primary caregiver, refused to be consistent. The school had repeatedly flagged Chirag's worsening behaviour, reminding his parents to seek mental health support. The interventions were started and stopped as the mother deemed fit. Basically, every time Chirag showed signs of improvement, the intervention would stop and he would fall back into his old habits.

The case of Vishal bears little resemblance to that of Chirag. But it perhaps exemplifies the threat that addiction poses for children, as also the increased risk to those lower on the socio-economic ladder. Of the sixteen years of his life, Vishal has been in and out of the system for the past nine. His first tryst with the child protection system was when he was produced before the CWC as a child of only seven. He ran away from school, and was caught committing petty theft. It was discovered that he was heavily under the influence of drugs. Vishal fell into the habit of consuming drugs when he was in grade 1. Ever since, he has been committing petty thefts to be able to buy drugs and alcohol. The classmate who introduced him to drugs lost his life to substance abuse. Vishal dropped out of school in grade 1 itself, and despite trying repeatedly, his father wasn't able to convince him to go back to school. Since then, he has done a number of odd jobs or petty crimes, mostly to be able to fund his drug addiction.

As I began putting this book together, my colleague at HAQ Vipin Bhatt reminded me of one of the most poignant cases that the team had worked on. It was also one of the most unique cases that the team has handled.

This was in the early days of our work with CICL. The killing of a child by an 8-year-old in one of Delhi's resettlement colonies in the mid-2000s scorched newspaper headlines. (Since the age of criminal responsibility in India is 7 years, the boy could be apprehended by the police.) The case was referred to the HAQ team. Vipin recalls that on his arrival at the Juvenile Justice Board (JJB), he was introduced to the 8-year-old, who appeared perplexed and terrified. He was escorted by the social workers of the OHB where he was placed.

He had been summoned by the JJB in order to hear his version of the incident directly from him. Slowly, he began to relax and respond to the friendly manner of the Principal Magistrate. The magistrate, a woman, in a very kind manner, asked the child to share his story.

The boy was from a village in Haryana. His father was a daily-wage labourer. The boy, we'll call him Monu, was in Delhi to meet some of his relatives. He and a neighbour, whom he had become friends with, were playing with a ball inside the home. As they played, the deceased child playfully gave Monu a push. Monu pushed him back—playfully. His friend fell back and his head hit the corner of the bed. He fell down dead. As he saw his friend lying on the floor he thought he was pretending. It was only when the boy just would not get up that he realized something serious had happened.

In an effort to understand the situation better, the magistrate probed a little further. She asked Monu if he and his friend had had a fight and that is why he had pushed him hard to hurt him. Monu said no. She further asked if he realized that his pushing his friend would kill him. Monu started crying. He simply repeated that they were playing and his friend had pushed him first and that he had only pushed him back. He had not thought that his friend would die. It was apparent that he was mortified by what had happened to his friend and then to him—his friend had *died* and he himself was picked up by the police and placed in an Observation Home, which in common parlance is often referred to as '*bachchon ka jail*' (children's jail).

The magistrate also enquired from the OHB's staff about Monu's behaviour in the Home. The staff told her that the child was very quiet, sad, non-communicative, cried intermittently, hardly ever ate and kept asking for his parents. He seemed completely at a loss. He just could not understand what had happened and why his friend had died, or even what his fault was.

Convinced that Monu had not intended to *kill* or harm his friend nor had attained the maturity to understand that a simple push could have such a grave consequence, the magistrate ordered Monu to be released. (She was convinced that this case was apt for a General Exception under Section 83 of the Indian Penal Code and that Monu ought to benefit from it.[8]) She sent the child back with his parents instructing them to ensure that Monu resumes his schooling as soon as possible. She made an additional order to HAQ to submit a home study and status-of-the-child report after a month to the JJB.

After a month, Bharti Ali and Vipin Bhatt made a home visit. Monu and his family lived in a two-room hut in a village in Haryana. Monu was in school. His father who was out working in the field, immediately dropped what he was doing and took Bharti and Vipin to the school. Vipin and Bharti instructed the father not to call Monu out of the class nor to point out to him. They decided to quietly observe him in his natural environment without making him conscious. They also gave the same instructions to the teacher. However, Monu looked up from whatever he was doing, recognized Vipin, looked fearful and began sweating. He was clearly traumatized by their presence.

Conversations with Monu's father and teacher told them that Monu had got back into his school routine and was well adjusted to the environment he was in. He was happy to be back with his family. But the sight of Vipin and Bharti had frightened him and had clearly triggered some bad memories.

In their report to the JJB, Bharti and Vipin, while explaining that Monu was doing well, also mentioned that seeing them was not good for his recovery and that hence they should avoid visiting him too often.

The system is not always able to fully deliver though, as it can be said to have done in the case of Monu. Bipasha Roy tells a similar story of a boy, a bright student, who had caused the death of his friend by hitting him below the ear with a rod. He broke down while talking to her and told her that the fight had started with a simple argument which led to both hitting each other with rods. Unfortunately, when he was about to hit his friend on the shoulder, the latter turned at the last moment and the blow fell at the base of his ear leading to his death. Did he intend to kill his friend? No. But the fact is that his friend had died and so he was in the system. The purpose of the juvenile justice system is to give the child a chance for a fresh start. To that extent, it is not meant to be punitive. Bipasha recalls that the Board, on assessment of the situation of the child (this was before the Amendment Act of 2015), decided to grant him bail so that he could continue schooling. However, at the time she retired, the case was six months old and was still pending, dangling over the young boy's head like an ever-present danger.

The greatest challenge that every one of us who works with the juvenile justice system faces is keeping the balance between being fair to both the CICL and the victim. There are some rare cases of gruesome murder or brutal sexual assault that have to be handled with care and sensitivity. Reflecting on her inner turmoil, Bipasha Roy says, 'While talking to a CICL, conflicting emotions would rage in me. I would be torn between detaining the offenders in the Observation Home and at the same time talking to them gently to assuage their fears and apprehensions. With experience I could control my emotions as the child's vulnerability and helplessness would soften my stance. I realized, after years of delving into the backgrounds of so many children, that most of them never got the opportunity of imbibing good values. Their life was a big struggle to survive. With no roof over their heads, or even the certainty of two square meals a day, often with no parents or guardians to take care of them…it was difficult, almost impossible grow into well-behaved, mature adults.'

What one finds when interacting with the children is that the effects of poverty are often compounded by peer influence. It has in fact been isolated by several studies as a major factor that predisposes offending children to criminal behaviour.[9] The fact that many among the children who end up in the system are in a severe state of deprivation only encourages the formation of gangs. It is through these gangs that the young people acquire criminal behaviour. It isn't hard to imagine why there is far higher likelihood of delinquency among young people belonging to a gang than those who are not.[10]

A young boy of about 8–10 years, we'll call him Sonu, along with another friend of 14–15 years, was having a good time till they were apprehended by the police. The mother of the young boy worked in a high-ranking civil servant's house as a maid and the father worked in a private company. Sonu and his friend, who also lived in the neighbourhood, would leave home every morning with their bags full of books, apparently headed for school. However, instead of going to school, they would walk around identifying houses where everyone had gone out. Perched on his older friend's shoulder, Sonu would enter the homes through windows or balconies. After stealing whatever small items they could carry in their bags, they would go to some scrap dealer, sell them and then buy guavas, ice cream, chocolate, etc., eat them and go back home.

The parents were both illiterate and too busy to ask about their school activities. Soon the boys felt more emboldened and started stealing more expensive things as well. The complaints in the neighbourhood about the thefts increased and the police were alerted. One day, as Sonu was trying to climb into a house through a kitchen window, perched on his friend's shoulder, the police arrived. The older boy ran away leaving Sonu to be caught by the police. Later, the older boy was caught too. There was a lot of pressure from the government officials whose houses had been stolen from by Sonu and his friend that they be 'punished'.

But the JJB magistrate, after hearing the details of the case, decided to have a 'chat' with the boys. They both pleaded guilty and promised that they would go back to school, upon which they were handed over to the parents.

'*Friendship thi, ma'am*' (It was friendship, ma'am), is how many children will describe what made them step into the world of crime. This was what was repeated to me in a recent visit to a Place of Safety (PoS) where the older boys are housed. Ranjan (name changed) could not hold back his tears, and nor could we. He was in school and was doing fairly well. He made friends with Kunal (name changed) who convinced him to pick pockets. On the fateful day they picked a fancy cellphone from someone's pocket. As luck would have it, the pocket was that of a police officer who managed to catch Ranjan. He said he had been taken to the police station and even tortured but he did not reveal Kunal's name. The reason? Kunal was not a very good student and was already behind in class. He was over 18 and if caught would be sent to adult prison. Ranjan did not wish that for him, so he took on the blame alone. His loyalty to his friend was moving. It also showed his strength of character. But his story also confirms how peer pressure, or 'friendship', remains one of the many reasons for children to get into the world of crime.

Richa Arora, in a report titled *Study of Children in Conflict with Law in Delhi*, which she wrote for TISS, spotlights residence as a key determinant of child delinquency. A child who witnesses crimes in his surroundings and neighbourhood becomes accustomed to such actions and learns from them. The area where the child lives, the surroundings and the socio-economic status of people around, play an important role in determining what the child is exposed to and what his/her actions might be.[11]

Jagdeep has been in and out of the system for a long time. Beginning with offences of lesser gravity, this time he was in for murder. It's his 'family honour' that he must protect, he said. He had in fact been convicted for not one but several murders, which he committed to save his family's 'honour' in a property dispute. When I met him, his older brother and father were in jail, and Jagdeep was in a PoS. It is quite clear that he does not think he did anything wrong, and nor does he think have his father and brothers. In fact, his family is proud of him.

One can only imagine how much worse it might be when the violence is not just in the surroundings but is directed specifically at the child.

Durga Meena's story, which was discussed in the previous chapter in the context of preliminary assessments made by JJBs, is a really sad one. She got married when she was 14 years old. At 17 she had, fed up with the violence she experienced at her husband's hands, picked up an axe and hit him, which led to his death. Her father-in-law was the witness. According to the order of the High Court, Durga's husband, Bherulal, not only beat her, he suspected that there were illicit relations between Durga and his father Unkar. He would beat her and 'also treated her like an animal every other day after consuming liquor'. On the night of 14 June 2016, Bherulal, under the influence of alcohol, assaulted Durga yet again, very badly this time. Thereafter, he poured kerosene on her body. But she ran away before he could set her on fire. The next night, Bherulal came home and thrashed her once again. Durga became infuriated. Unable to contain her exasperation and anger, she picked up an axe and landed a blow to the inebriated Bherulal's head. A single blow with the axe proved fatal, and Durga was apprehended and tried for murder.[12]

Growing up amid violence, especially domestic violence, can affect children even when they are not the immediate victims. And even a moment of anger can lead to grave and long-lasting consequences for them. In one of the early cases that HAQ was involved in, we met Quasim (name changed), who had been in the Observation Home for several years. He had no legal representation and hence had never got bail. It was hard to believe that such a gentle boy had killed his own father. It turned out that the father would return home drunk every night and beat his mother. The boy had stood by helplessly for a long time. Like in the case of Durga, there came a night when he couldn't bear it any longer. Quasim pulled his father away as he hit his mother and pushed him hard. High on alcohol, and with no control over his body, the father fell against the wall, hit his head and died. The boy was charged with murder, apprehended and kept incarcerated—almost forgotten until a lawyer visiting the Observation Home found him. He was finally released with his years in the Observation Home treated as conviction undergone.

But there are a myriad other ways in which families can affect their young, and interventions need to be tailored to suit the child. Jasmeet (name changed) was sent to us for counselling because she had created a bomb scare by dialling 100 and lying to the police. This was just before Independence Day and there was a high alert in the whole city of Delhi. It is not hard to imagine what a phone call like this could do. Of course, it turned out to be a hoax. The call was traced to Jasmeet, and she was apprehended (children are apprehended and not arrested in the JJ Act).

Her father would drive her to the HAQ office for her sessions. Slowly, we managed to make some headway and the story became clearer. Jasmeet had a young brother—much younger than her, the long-awaited male child born after much prayer. Following his birth, Jasmeet, who up until then was the only child, began to feel neglected and unwanted. The boy was the centre of everybody's attention. And this was her way of seeking it for herself. It took several sessions with Jasmeet alone, with her and her parents together, and a change of school for Jasmeet to slowly become the child she wished to be.

On 10 January 2020, *Hindustan Times* reported:

> The 17-year, 361-day old young man, behind the wheel of his father's speeding Mercedes Benz, who hit and killed

marketing professional Siddharth Sharma, 32 on April 4, 2016, will not go to jail for his crime with the Supreme Court ruling on Thursday that the act of the accused, a juvenile at the time of the commission of the offence, does not fall within the category of 'heinous offences' under the Juvenile Justice Act, 2015.

Under the Act, only juveniles committing 'heinous crimes' are to be tried as adults. The boy's lawyer said that had this been a case of a hit and run by an adult truck driver, he would have been charged under the Motor Vehicles Act, 1988 (this case was before the amendment of the law in 2019 which now says 'Where an offence under this Act has been committed by a juvenile, then such juvenile shall be punishable with such fines as provided in the Act while any custodial sentence may be modified as per the provisions of the Juvenile Justice Act, 2000' [Section 86 (6)]). As an adult he would have got one to three years of imprisonment.[13] There was, of course, no provision for dealing with children in that law.

Shilpa Sharma, the victim's sister, said that she 'is devastated by the ruling but will continue her fight for justice'.[14] Her grief is understandable. The death of Siddharth Sharma was tragic, and the action of the boy and his parents who allowed him to drive their car, irresponsible and indulgent.

But would sending this boy into prison for life, or hanging him, be the solution? Can it be assumed that the boy did not feel any remorse?

The same rage that was expressed in the case of the 'juvenile' in the Nirbhaya case was witnessed once more with the public demanding that this boy be treated as an adult and punished as an adult. It has been several years and all that's happening in the case is that it is moving from court to court. What he did was really terrible. But the retribution is dragging on and on. His life is at a standstill with no future in sight. Unable to plan a life for himself, it has affected his mental health as well as that of the family, who now live lives of uncertainty.

Rohan's life was one lived on the streets after he was orphaned at age 11, losing his parents in quick succession. His three married brothers and two married sisters could offer him no familial or emotional anchoring or education. An existence on the street became a way of life for him. This was around Delhi's Jama Masjid area and the bylanes of Meena Bazar. He was arrested for theft, lodged in an Observation Home and recommended counselling. He was about 14 or 15 years old by then. During his sessions he boasted about his addiction to psychotropic substances in the form of tablets and also to sniffing shoe polish and having sex with multiple partners. In fact, in his counselling sessions, his counsellor reported that he was too preoccupied with describing his sexual exploits. He called his sexual liaisons 'settings' and often went into lurid details. He had scant respect for or attachments with these women/girls. And none of them lingered in his life.

After one of the sessions with him, his counsellor, a colleague of mine, described him as being sullen and silent, refusing to speak. When asked why, he confessed to being attracted to her and fantasizing about her. He wanted that she be intimate with him, that she become his 'setting'. Trying to divert him through games, or explaining to him that this was a professional relationship and that it is possible for boys and girls to be friends without intimacy, did not persuade him. He dismissed her arguments and demanded that she understand him and fulfil his needs. This behaviour continued over several sessions. When the counsellor did not respond, he began banging his head on the wall. The counsellor surmised that this was not the first time he had done that as she had noticed scars on his forehead before.

Explaining his behaviour, his counsellor concluded that Rohan had been deprived of traditional bonds in his infancy and growing-up years, be it with his parents or siblings, and it precluded him from building healthier relations based on love and trust. He grew up with little understanding of his own emotions or the feelings of others. It limited his ability to build or maintain successful relationships. His trysts with the opposite sex were not emotional bonding, but meant only to be transitory in nature. That was all he knew relationships to be. While intimacy required commitment, something he knew nothing about, objectifying was an easy, familiar road for him, one that gave him moments of connection and pleasure but ruled out potential rejection. And rejection was something he dreaded, having been abandoned by his family.

Examination of reports on child offenders shows that among the many reasons for why they commit violent crimes is the lack of self-esteem and parental support. And this cuts across class lines. But there is almost always a trigger.

On 20 December 2017, there was a story[15] of a 16-year-old teenager who had confessed to having killed his mother and sister in their fourteenth-floor apartment in Greater Noida with a cricket bat and then disfiguring their faces with a pair of scissors and a pizza cutter. According to the news report, the boy was often scolded by his parents over his low grades in school and had a fierce rivalry with his sister, a class six student, who was outstanding in her studies. It is alleged that his parents used to cite her as an example to belittle him and he thought his parents did not love him, police added. The immediate trigger for the murders was his mother scolding and beating him on the afternoon of 4 December. Having committed the murders he ran away, but was confused with what had happened and began missing his father. That is when he was caught.

In another incident, 8-year-old Pradyuman Thakur was found dead in the school toilet of Ryan International School in Gurugram in November 2017. There were reports that a 16-year-old boy had allegedly taken this extreme step in hopes of postponing the semester exams and the parent–teacher meeting that was planned.[16] The following details emerged about the alleged offender: the father was a lawyer in Gurugram and one of the wealthy individuals of the area owning properties of over Rs 500 crore; his parents fought constantly and he was troubled by these fights. There were also reports of the behavioural problems that he displayed. He watched porn, and his classmates are said to have reported that he had a 'vulgar character' and showed 'rude behaviour' in school.[17] Another classmate claimed, 'He was not so good in education and sports.' But while he was bad at studies, he was good at playing the piano. His neighbours too spoke about his behavioural issues. 'He used to behave normally with others but would get furious when someone called him fat or bulky,' a resident of his colony said, adding that locals generally avoided the teen.[18]

The child was apprehended and the case is currently sub judice. Taking cognizance of the matter, on 13 July 2022, the Supreme Court had again sent the matter to the Gurugram JJB for review to decide whether the CICL should be treated as an adult or a minor.

On 27 July, the Board sought an opinion from its empanelled psychiatrist. Later, three psychiatrists from PGI Rohtak submitted a report. In the report, it was submitted that 'Bholu (name changed), as of today, has the maturity to understand the alleged offence, but no valid conclusion can be drawn. Due to many inconsistencies in Bholu's old reports and assessments, no valid conclusion can be drawn as to what would be [*sic*] his state of mind at the time of the incident.' Based on this report and a private conversation with him, the JJB, on 17 October 2022, ordered that he be tried as an adult.

On 20 October, the Division Bench of the Supreme Court comprising Justices Dinesh Maheshwari and J.K. Maheshwari granted the boy interim bail. They noted that he had already been in a correctional facility for five years. Justice Maheshwari said, 'You are looking at only the emotions, and not the reality. The crime is barbaric and horrifying. But still, the law must have balance.'[19]

The concerns and questions, however, remain. The impending examinations and the parent–teacher meeting were clearly the immediate triggers for his action. That he had a troubled childhood, showed behavioural problems and was undergoing psychiatric treatment is also something to be noted. But what kind of distress must he have been suffering for him to take such a drastic step? Again, would punishing him like an adult be enough? Besides, can he be tried as an adult when the psychiatric report is inconclusive? Can his current frame of mind be indicative of what it was when the incident took place five years ago and he was much younger?

It is apparent to all of us who work among the children in child care institutions how, for these children, the process *is* the punishment. As Justice Madan Lokur often says, the children are treated as spectators in the process of their own case. No one talks to them or listens to them; they simply are numbers in the justice system.

In 2020, standing in front of Rocky (name changed), all I saw was a young adult who was very quiet and yet wanted to talk. I did not ask him very much as he explained his art work to me. This was at an open house organized by Yuva Ekta Foundation at a PoS in Delhi. The images he had drawn, the colours he had used, reflected his mental state—I could sense his desperation and anxiety. And yet Rocky did not quite 'fit'—he seemed different. The pain in his eyes was palpable. He had a quiet aloofness about him. Curious, I asked the Yuva Ekta team about him.

'Remember the dancer who was supposed to have murdered to get money so he could participate in a dance reality show?' he asked me. Yes, I did remember, but I also went back to read the news story, and put a name to the face. While what he had allegedly done was horrendous and real, what one could see in Rocky that day was also just as real. According to the newspaper report,[20] while Rocky's father had accepted the truth, his mother was still living in denial. Quoting his mother the newspaper reported, 'He could not even remove a dead rat from the house, how could he kill two persons? When I go meet him at the correction home now, he just hangs his head and cries.' Rocky was being tried by the JJB. His family says he has changed. However, what has not changed is his love for dance. Although he seemed to have stopped by the time I met him, as per the report, he had started teaching dance to other juveniles lodged in the correction home.

The next time I went to the PoS, Rocky was not there. I was informed he was on parole based on a Supreme Court order to decongest homes during the Covid pandemic. But in 2022, I found him back again in the institution. He had returned himself once his parole was over. While on parole he was working with his father in his father's air-conditioner repair shop. He even ensured that other boys coming out of the juvenile justice system got employed by his father.

It's been seven years since Rocky first entered the system. He is now an adult. In the meantime, he has completed his schooling from the open schooling system. He offers himself for any training options available to the inmates. But he has no idea what stage his case is in. As per the law, there should have been an assessment when he turned 21 and a decision made as to whether he could be released based on his record. That has not happened. His father has already spent a fair amount of money on a private lawyer, who has done little to move the case forward.

The latest information received is that the High Court has rejected his bail application. Yes, it's true that the crime Rocky had committed was horrendous and grave. But just as Justice Maheshwari remarked in the Gurugram case, 'the law must have balance'.

Rocky is not the only one. Walking through the facility, I found many boys who were no longer boys—they were grown men who had been there for years and years. They just laze about, bully and abuse others, filled with anger and mistrust. The superintendent tells me that if they were to be released, some of them, particularly those that are members of gangs, would just as easily slide back into violence. But he was torn, because he wasn't sure if the solution was to keep them locked up inside a juvenile facility. There's little to be done though. As long as a case is pending in court the inmates remain where they are. Bored and unfit for the real world, if and when they are sent out.

As always, it is those that live in poverty who are dealt the worst hand. Bipasha Roy recounts to me what an inmate once told her: 'Ma'am, I was begging in the food stalls for a scrap of food, I begged to the customers to give me some food but I was shooed away. No one came forward to help me. I also tried to get some work but people would tell me to go away. I had to steal to survive. What would you have done in my place?' That child had been abandoned by his parents. He stole and sold scraps from a tram depot in Kolkata to survive.

Mental health is only beginning to be recognized as a problem. And yet, instead of looking at mental health services as a supportive intervention, they are being used for preliminary assessments to determine the capacity of a child to commit an offence! According to the Indian Council for Medical Research, one in seven persons in India have mental health issues.[21] It is only legitimate to ask, in any and every case of an offending child, how, in the absence of a comprehensive mental health assessment, we can ever know what the cause of an action by a child is.

I met a boy once who had been apprehended for a very brutal murder of a woman in front of her young child. After much deliberation and conversations with the family, the boy was given bail. The JJB was clearly not fully equipped to understand the mental status of this boy. They relied on reports from counsellors who visit the Special Home.

Within three months into the bail, he was apprehended again for murder, this time of his friend, and in exactly the same manner. Is simply sending this boy into the adult system, which is what is bound to happen now, the only solution? I would think this boy needs serious help. In fact, that is what he seems to be crying out for.

Ashim wanted to be kept in a separate lock-up, away from all the other boys. When I met him, he was sharing his cell with another boy. His cell was neat and clean. He had collected all the sheets, towels and toiletries he had received and arranged them in a neat pile—colour coded. It was a huge stock. He was hoarding what was given to him. There was clearly some reason that no one from his family wanted to come and take him or push his case.

These are examples of children and adolescents who are emotionally unstable and unaware of the triggers. Even though I am part of the Delhi State Selection Committee for JJB and CWC members, I am aware that the JJB members themselves are not fully equipped to assess the kind of support they need to order. They are too busy interpreting sections of the law and what they must do.

But the neglect of mental health doesn't merely pose a problem in dealing with CICL who might need psychiatric help or psycho-social support. It is, more broadly, a matter of providing children with the opportunity to express themselves, to tell us about their hopes and worries without fear of punishment. It is a question of letting children know that even if they do make mistakes, the system exists not to punish them but to help them reform and be the best version of themselves.

On 8 May 2020, a 16-year-old boy jumped off the eleventh floor of his apartment building and died. As per reports, he was deeply troubled by the public shaming on social media after a girl posted that he had molested her when he was 14 years old.[22] We will never know his side of the story because he is dead. And we only have the girl's version. He may have indeed behaved inappropriately. This is an offence. And if he had done so, the girl had every right to complain. Perhaps it was the fear of being branded a sex offender for life that drove him to jump. A member of his extended family got in touch with me. They were distraught and confused. His parents wanted the girl who had made the post on Instagram arrested and punished. If they succeed, that will be yet another CICL in the system.

If only the girl had found the courage and the safe space to seek justice instead of Instagram! If only both he and the girl had spoken to someone—maybe, just maybe, he would be alive today, with the opportunity for a fresh start in life.

Many would be quick to conclude that the boy 'got what he deserved', without realizing what we all stand to lose with such an unforgiving stance towards young people.

I am often asked why I am so incensed when children who could be 'threats to security', even national security, or 'criminals' are 'picked up' or 'detained'. After all it is well known that adolescents have been part of stone pelting, rioting and other 'anti-national' activities. Even a court reminded us of this when hearing a case we had presented before it. Besides, they ask me, what defence is there for supporting children who commit really serious and horrendous offences?

It is true that many of them are involved in agitations and may also have, at times, pelted stones and resorted to violence. But who is engaging with them to 'hear' them? To find out what their concerns are. Instead, what one hears is statements like the one made by late General Bipin Rawat, former Chief of Defence Staff, who spoke of sending children to 'de-radicalization' camps.[23] Again, will simply institutionalizing children solve the problem?

The last few months of 2019 and 2020 saw children being detained for being part of the CAA-NRC protests, against the introduction of the Citizenship (Amendment) Act and the proposed implementation of the National Register of Citizens.

HAQ, along with the Quill Foundation and Citizens Against Hate, undertook a fact-finding effort. What we found was bloodcurdling. In the report published in January 2020 titled *Brutalising Innocence: Detention, Torture & Criminalisation of Minors by UP Police to Quell Anti-CAA Protests*, one finds that close to forty-one minors faced detention and custodial torture. Of these, twenty-two minors were detained and tortured in Bijnor and fourteen in Muzaffarnagar. In the case of the latter, FIRs had been filed against four who were released after twelve days. All detained minors that the fact-finding team spoke to testified that they were beaten with police batons/lathis and made to witness violence inflicted by police on detained adults. Tortured children returned home with bruised body parts and fractures. Whether or not one agrees with the politics they came out in support of, is that how the system ought to be treating these children, as hardened criminals who will never reform?

It is true that despite all efforts there may still be children who may never change. Crime and the world of crime are ingrained in them. Despite spending years in a reform facility they keep coming back. Rajeev was one such boy. He was part of a gang who were involved in violence and looting. The last time I saw him, he himself chose to stay in isolation—so great were his anger issues. I found out later that he had got bail. But instead of leading a low-profile life on the right side of the law, he picked a fight. This time because he was jealous. And he had cut his girlfriend's cheek with a blade to teach her a lesson—landing him now in adult prison as he had crossed 18 years.

But because there may be a Rajeev, must we give up on all children? Instead of creating an 'other', if we can only admit that *all* children at some point have the capacity to break the law, our demand would not be for more and more punitive laws and punishment. It might be for an opportunity to reform and for a fresh start for these children. That is what the spirit—and even the letter—of our law on juvenile justice demands.

5

THOSE WHO NEVER GIVE UP
ON CHILDREN

We read in the papers and hear on the air
Of killing and stealing and crime everywhere
We sigh and say as we notice the trend,
This young generation where will it end?
But can we be sure it's their fault alone
Are we less guilty who place in their way
Too many things that lead them astray
Kids don't make the movies,
They don't write the books
They don't paint gay pictures
of gangsters and crooks
They don't make the liquor,
and they don't run the bars
They don't make the laws
and they don't make the cars
They don't make the drugs that muddle the brain
That's done by older folks greedy for gain
Delinquent teenagers, oh how we condemn
For the sins of the nation and blame it on them
By the laws of the blameless
'Someone' made known

Who is there among us to cast the first stone
For in some many cases, it's sad but it's true
The title delinquent fits older folks too

— 'Who's to Blame?', written by Judge Angelo D.
Malandra, Juvenile and Domestic Relations Court,
Camden County, New Jersey, USA

One of the best chroniclers of the history of juvenile justice in India is undoubtedly Prof Ved Kumari. She is an undying believer in the capacity of the young offender to reform and the need to have a separate system for children who come in conflict with the law. I have attended her lectures, been on panel discussions with her in seminars and workshops, watched her trainings and even had the privilege of conducting a session with her.

She invariably takes the participants back to their childhood and asks them to recall if they have ever done anything which, had they been 'caught', would have constituted an offence. As is to be expected, there is seldom anyone who can say he or she never did any such thing. But what they describe never constitutes what is popularly called a 'serious offence'. That's when the narrative gets all garbled and muddy.

Talking about this, Ved Kumari says, 'The tension becomes palpable when a plea of juvenility is raised by a defendant charged with serious offences. This situation can be viewed as an attempt to *take advantage* of the juvenile justice system, and not as the exercise of a recognized right of the child.'

Explaining this dilemma, she cites the example of Ajmal Kasab, who had been convicted and then hanged for his involvement in the terrorist attack on the Taj Hotel and other places in Mumbai, which killed hundreds of people. Ajmal

Kasab had at one stage raised the defence of being a child on the date of offence. She says, 'His plea was rejected, as he was not found to be a child. However, it did raise a crucial question: how many of us would have been comfortable if Kasab had indeed been a child on the date of the terrorist attack?'[1]

Clearly, most of the country would have been deeply uncomfortable. They were much more comfortable at his being hanged, as they would have been if a similar fate had been meted out to the juvenile who was named as an accused in the Nirbhaya case. Even after the four adults were hanged, people felt that full justice had not been done as the 'juvenile got away'.

Because most of us see the offence and not the offender, it becomes important to dedicate a chapter to all those people who do not give up on children, those who trust and believe that they can reform and make a fresh start, and are willing to work towards that. Although a minority, given the huge numbers who are on the other side, they do exist. And it is because they do that children get a chance.

Had Vasudha Dhagamwar, for example, not stood up for the four Pahadiya boys in 1980, their case would never have come up before the Supreme Court, and they might have still been languishing in prison.

Had Advocate Anup Bhambhani (now judge in the Delhi High Court) not represented the minor and advocate Vrinda Grover the intervening organizations in *Dr Subramanian Swamy and Ors vs Raju*, we would not have got the landmark judgement that we did from the Supreme Court of India. (There were several well-known lawyers who had refused to represent the minor in this case, and in fact even refused to be the advocate-on-record!)

There are many like them, spread across the country and around the globe. It wouldn't be possible for me to include the stories of all of them here. I must therefore include only a few examples. These are academics, judicial officers, lawyers or have worked with or on juvenile justice, and have mentored many others like themselves. They are individuals who give us hope for the future.

Ved Kumari's interest in juvenile justice dates back to before the start of her professional career—to 1978, when she was doing her LLM. When Professor Upendra Baxi, her guide, suggested that it was important to understand the context of the law, she decided to step out and acquaint herself with the workings of the juvenile justice system. Her interactions with children, who are the subject of this law, and also the subject of her dissertation, and the stories she heard helped her understand whether and how the law is being implemented. As she says, 'I think once you interact with a child, it's very difficult not to think about them after your official dissertation is over.'[2]

Ved Kumari is one of the exceptions who went seeking to work with children who offend. For most, it suddenly 'happens' for them. They either find themselves 'appointed' for the job or meander into it unknowingly and never give up.

One such individual was Father Placido Fonseca, a Jesuit priest, and director of the orphanage Snehasadan in Mumbai since 1970, who passed away in 2021 at the age of 84. He always believed that the child is never wrong. As a result, he insisted on no background checks for any child coming or sent to Snehasadan. 'We *adults* are wrong in the way we have communicated with him or her, hurting and upsetting the child,' is what he would tell Sangeeta Punekar who worked with him since 1988 till he passed away. It was what he expected every social worker in his team to believe, she says. Snehasadan is designed as an open facility. There has never been a lock and key there. It is designed to run on trust. If a child ran away, Father Placie, as he was better known, would send off his social workers to find them and bring them back. But he never judged them for what they may have done—although many found themselves on the wrong side of the law while living on the streets or on railway platforms.

Amin Sheikh describes his life and journey in *Bombay, Mumbai. Life is life. I Am Because of You* (2016). He grew up in Snehasadan. Reading his story, one cannot help but be astonished how many times he barely escaped being arrested. Had the team of Snehasadan not believed in him, given him the chance for a fresh start, he could have ended up among the countless nameless, faceless CICL of India.

Advocate Maharukh Adenwalla is passionate often to the point of being obdurate when it comes to issues around juvenile justice. But one cannot but love her for it. She will fight tooth and nail for 'her boys' or 'her girls' because she believes that each one of them needs another chance. Has she never felt let down by her 'boys'? we ask her. 'Of course, I have,' she responds. 'But just because of that one, should I give up on the others? Nevvver,' she says in her distinct Parsi accent!

Maharukh is from Mumbai—born in Mumbai and has lived in it her entire life. She has been a human rights advocate 'all her life'. I first met her in 1996. She was then part of the Human Rights Law Network team. Whatever the disappointments in court, or the behaviour of her clients, her commitment to human rights remained unwavering. '*Kuch bhi ho, appan ko to kanoon ka neechu mein aana haayich na?*' she will remind us. (Whatever happens has to be as per the rule of law, according to the tenets of law.) This book will never be complete without the story of my friend Maharukh.

Like me, Maharukh too happened to read the Juvenile Justice Act, 1986 for the first time in 1990s. It made her keen to understand the functioning of the juvenile justice system, more particularly, the Observation Home,[3] which under that Act housed both neglected juveniles (children in need of care and protection) and juvenile delinquents (children in conflict with the law), before they were separated and placed in different homes or institutions. Just as in Delhi, in Mumbai too (Bombay then), gaining entry into the premises of the Observation Home was very difficult. Not knowing how to do so, it was shelved as a 'future task'.

This 'future task' fructified at a social gathering a couple of weeks later. Maharukh was at a friend's dinner party and started chatting with a woman who turned out to be the deputy secretary of the Department of Women and Child Development, Government of Maharashtra, which had very recently been set up. As she says, 'If that is not "luck-by-chance", I don't know what is.' The deputy secretary fixed up a meeting between Maharukh and her boss, the secretary of the Department. The secretary was truly pro-active. She immediately issued a letter of permission. Not just that, she actually called the superintendent of the Observation Home and ordered that Maharukh be allowed entry into the Home. Thus started her journey in juvenile justice.

She started spending most Mondays at the Observation Home where in the morning she would provide legal assistance to the juvenile welfare board, and spend the afternoons with the girls in the child guidance clinic holding sessions on law with them.

Although the girls were happy to meet her once a week, because she was a lawyer, most were interested in knowing what she could do to get them out of the Observation Home, which they perceived as a prison. In fact, it *was* prison-like—a closed institution, encompassed by high walls and situated on the erstwhile 'Jail Road'.

Maharukh recounts that during this period she learned two crucial lessons—firstly, that no matter what facilities and amenities were offered in the Observation Home, children wanted to walk out of its doors at the earliest; secondly, the juvenile justice system was personality-driven, its efficacy depended on the traits of individual functionaries. If they were kind and enterprising, children received better care; if not, children suffered.

There was yet another lesson she learned during those early days. One of the girls she met was in the Observation Home for theft. She says, 'This was my first matter before the Juvenile Court, which then used to sit for half a day every Friday. More than my arguments before the Juvenile Court, it was persuading the mother that was back-breaking... I realized that if I wanted to work in the juvenile justice system, I would be required to play roles other than that of a lawyer, especially in the 1990s, when there were very few professionals working with juvenile delinquents.'[4]

She recounted to me a case where her tasks went beyond simply securing the child's release to ensuring his physical well-being as well. 'I recall a child ["X"] against whom there were several cases of theft pending before the Board (he used to steal iron gutter-lids and sell them). Completion of enquiries would have taken years, and his family was in another State, hence, bail was not an option. I decided to seek discharge on the ground that he had spent a long time in the Observation Home. But just then we came to know that X had a hole in his heart, which required surgery. So in consultation with the superintendent of the Observation Home and X's family, he was successfully operated in a public hospital while under the state's charge. It is only later that I got X discharged and he returned home with his father, who I remember had the face of a saint in a medieval painting.'

It was her colleague, Dr Yug Mohit Chaudhry, who as a trial lawyer in the sessions court had come across several children within the criminal justice system who expressly requested that she represent them. 'Hence, in the early 2000s, in order to understand the working of the 2000 Act, I applied to the legal services authority to be appointed as a legal-aid lawyer in the Observation Home, and I was so appointed for three consecutive years. I used to make applications before the magistrate's courts, the sessions court and the High Court to return children who were wrongly treated as adults into the juvenile justice system. Once they were so returned, I would appear on their behalf before the Juvenile Justice Board (JJB). Most of them had no support in Mumbai and bail could not be availed of. Thus, my focus was on expeditious completion of their enquiries before the Board. During those three years, there were so many child clients that I became friends with—some of whom I am presently in contact with. Appearing on their behalf was important.'

She realized during her stint as a legal-aid lawyer that it is important to recognize that every case of children in conflict with the law requires a distinct intervention—every child's need differs—and if the objective of juvenile justice legislation is to be fulfilled, the functionaries of the juvenile justice system, including the lawyer, have to be creative in deploying the law and the system in the interest of the child. That is why, even as she represents children, she is engaged in training, teaching and advocacy for better systems. Having worked through the lacunae and defects in the Juvenile Justice Act, 2000, and the subsequent amendments, to implement the legislation in its true spirit, she has constantly advocated for improvements in the law.

Despite the challenges that the juvenile justice system poses, Maharukh's commitment to providing support to children who may have come in conflict with the law remains unwavering. 'A child requires protection due to his or her stage of mental and physical development. I never faced a dilemma in representing a child in conflict with the law who had harmed another child—I understood that the child had acted so due to his mental immaturity, and required positive inputs and measures to bring a positive change in him. I know that this is possible—I have never witnessed otherwise in all these years.'

She acknowledges the changes since she first started working on juvenile justice in the 1990s. 'There are more organizations and individuals working—children benefit from such contact and intervention, not only within the Observation Homes or Special Homes, but also once they are in a community-setting,' she says. But she remains concerned about the future because she has watched children floundering in the criminal justice system at the hands of lawyers and judges who treat them as any other accused, particularly after the introduction of the possibility of transfer to the adult system in the JJ Act, 2015. Much of her energy now goes into ensuring that a child is retained within the juvenile justice system or restored to it.

'I have returned to the Juvenile Justice Board to represent children during preliminary assessments—attempting to persuade the Board not to transfer a child. Before the sessions court and High Court, I attempt to raise each provision of the juvenile justice legislation to the advantage of the child, and challenge provisions that are detrimental to their interests.' She adds, 'Removing a child from the ameliorative effect of the juvenile justice system brings me much pain.'

For Bipasha Roy, whose observations I've shared in previous chapters, it all started with visiting a children-cum-Observation Home for Girls way back in 2006 as part of an NGO which would send its members for rendering voluntary service in the Home. She had volunteered to coach the children in elementary English. Initially, the visit would entail a two- to three-hour-long tutoring of children in learning the alphabet and phonetics. However, slowly she found herself getting involved in settling quarrels between the girls, listening to their problems and learning about their lives. Since it was a children-cum-OHG, it housed both CNCP and CICL. But there was a hierarchy established among them based on which category they belonged to. While the 'CNCP girls' were allowed to move around within the Home and the compound and attend classes, she never met the 'CICL girls'. As she says, 'That's when the gross disparity in handling a CNCP and a CICL by the child care institutions came fully to my attention. It was that feeling of witnessing something so unfair which nudged me into applying for and then joining the Juvenile Justice Board of Kolkata as its member.'

Even to this day she distinctly remembers her first day as a member of the JJB. The Board was meeting in the chamber of the Principal Magistrate in Bankshall Court, she recalls.

A boy aged about 12–13 years was ushered in by the police (in uniform). He had been apprehended for trying to steal an endangered species of bird from Alipore Zoo (Kolkata). 'My theoretical knowledge of the JJ Act had not prepared me for talking to a child who had been traumatized by the apprehension, the handling of the police, ferried by strangers in a police van to an unknown destination to meet some more strangers.' She found fear and helplessness writ large on the child's face.

Soon the parents of the boy arrived with a lawyer they had hired by expending their meagre means, oblivious to the fact that they had the right to apply for free legal aid. The child, through his tears, had only one thing to say, 'Please don't send me away, I want to go home.' Bipasha recalls, 'Thus began my long and arduous journey into the world of vulnerable children where they taught me more than I could ever teach them. They taught me resilience, hope, bonding, honesty, survival fighting all odds, trust and laughter. They also taught me to value things that we take for granted.'

But she makes another point. 'I was never in doubt that when the layers of misery, abuse, trauma and mistrust were peeled away with unconditional love and hand-holding, in terms of a good rehabilitation package and follow-up, each child would bloom into a beautiful human being. There is never a requirement for a reassessment to try a CICL as an adult. It's for us to help them re-live and enjoy their childhood and not push them to an early adulthood.'

Advocate Chandra Suman's lack of legal briefs became his reason to begin work with CICL—which soon turned into a vocation and passion. In 2008, a senior lawyer introduced him to Ms Minna Kabir, a passionate child rights activist who had set up a legal support programme for young people accused of committing offences. Since then he has been working closely with CICL, representing them in the JJBs. In 2021, he was appointed as a member of a JJB. He says, 'My first challenge was to overcome my own prejudices regarding the child offenders. Working so closely with child offenders as their legal-aid counsel, I came to know about their family conditions, and their social environments and daily struggles. That's how the realization struck me that child delinquency is not a legal issue but rather a social issue.'[5]

During the heated discussions on the government's proposal to change the law and make children culpable for heinous crimes (leading to the 2015 amendment), I recall Chandra Suman saying, 'If a mother has two sons, and one pokes the other in the eye making him blind, what will the mother do? Will she poke the "offending" son in the eye and make him blind too? Or worse, what if it led to death? Will she kill the son who killed his brother? Is that the solution?' He was trying to explain why more and more punitive measures were not the solution for addressing crimes by children.

Based on his work over the years, Chandra Suman asserts, 'After 12 years of my experience of working with child offenders, I can say that only about 8–10 per cent of CICL are repeat offenders and the rest can be rehabilitated into society as good citizens. We really can't blame the 90 per cent for the fault of the 10 per cent. We must realize what a great success it would be for the society and system if we were to rehabilitate the former even if we can't reform the latter.'

In 2012, Sachi Maniar, a young filmmaker, had only gone to paint the walls of a Children's Home in Mumbai as part of a group of volunteers. Little did she realize that she would never leave. She founded Ashiyana, an NGO which works with children in Dongri in Mumbai, which houses both a Children's Home as well as an Observation Home. She began by working with children who need care and protection. One day, a boy who was a CICL was transferred to the Children's Home from the Observation Home. This was her first interaction with a child who had offended. Since then there has been no looking back.

Her days are spent giving hope to children, and sometimes to their parents who have given up on them. Sachi has got herself trained in restorative justice processes so that she can serve these children better. She and her team teach them to paint, garden, study for exams—but most importantly, she teaches them to believe in themselves.

At a webinar on 21 July 2020, when she was describing how she and the Ashiyana team take the boys out of the Home for performances on stage or for treks and picnics, someone asked, 'What if they run away?'

'We trust them,' replied Sachi. 'We tell them that we trust them. Once they know that, they do not run.'

Kalpana Purushothaman, a trained psychologist, was working in the corporate sector after a few initial years of her career as a counsellor and an academic. For years, on weekends, she would volunteer with different NGOs working for different causes under various organizational corporate social responsibility programmes. By her own admission, she knew nothing about juvenile justice. She was merely offering counselling and life skills to some children in a slum. Had it not been for the fact that a young boy, Manish, who attended her classes, got 'picked up' by the police, and had his mother not sought her help to 'speak [in] English' to the police, she would have remained oblivious. Manish was found dead in a ditch a few days later. This woke her up to what happens to children who get 'picked up' by the police as offenders. Since then, she has supported CICL as a counsellor and has been a JJB member in Bangalore. She shares her experiences in Part 2 of this book.

But like myself, these are all people who, though they meandered into this world, did so by their choice. There are some who are part of the system that are there because it is their 'job'.

As Premoday Khakha says, 'A public servant has no choice as it is the government which decides what responsibility is to be assigned to him.' However, an academic background, keenness to explore and learn, past performance and experiences do count when taking up such assignments for an individual given the responsibility. These must have been of help to him when he was posted as superintendent-in-charge of the Observation Home for Boys (OHB) in Delhi that housed children above 16 years of age. 'For me, the objective was clear. "*Sazaa nahin, disha*" (direction, not punishment) was my driving factor. And I have worked to initiate action that focused on the living environment that the institution provided and set up a communication system with a child placed in my protective custody.'

'Working with them made me a more tolerant person. Working with children in conflict with the law confirmed my belief that they are victims of circumstance and were indeed children who were also in need of care and protection,' says Ratna Saxena, who served as the superintendent of Prayas

Home for Boys, Delhi for many years. She shares how her 'job' transformed her as a human being: 'My professionalism was tested repeatedly as I worked to implement the provisions of the JJ Act, especially with children who were alleged to have committed heinous offences. When I began there were conflicts within me, between my own principles and those of juvenile justice. I'm only too happy that the principles set out in the JJ Act won, and in turn became my principles too. I am now of the firm belief that the stories of failure we hear are not about the failure of the children—they're about the failure of the system.'

Justice Madan B. Lokur was the first chairperson of the first Juvenile Justice Committee of the Delhi High Court. Now, most High Courts have a juvenile justice committee. He was also the first chairperson of the Supreme Court Juvenile Justice Committee. According to him, the key moment of change in his life was brought on by his appointment as the chairperson of the first juvenile justice committee set up in the Delhi High Court in 2006. Till then he had little interest in 'juvenile delinquents' or the juvenile justice law. He had never needed to deal closely with either. Indeed, he can barely recall the habeas corpus petition before him in the Delhi High Court that HAQ had filed when Ramesh had gone missing—the boy who had been picked up by the police and sent to Tihar Jail.

As he says, 'Sometime in 2006, the then Chief Justice of India seems to have received a complaint about the not-so-good condition of children in homes across the country. He wrote a letter to the chief justices perhaps of all the High Courts to nominate a committee to improve the condition of these homes. The chief justice of the Delhi High Court acted upon the letter and nominated me for that purpose.'

I still remember that evening when he called me up to tell me of his appointment. We discussed what this entailed and what I knew of the system. This was also the year in which Ruzbeh Bharucha was volunteering with HAQ, visiting child care institutions and documenting what he saw. Ruzbeh too met Justice Lokur and shared his experiences.

Soon after being appointed, Justice Lokur decided to visit the OHB in Kingsway Camp in Delhi. What he saw completely shocked him. There were four dormitories each for twenty-five children. Instead of the 100 children it was meant for, there were 258 children living there awaiting conclusion of the proceedings before the JJB. In other words, the enquiry under the Juvenile Justice (Care and Protection of Children) Act was pending and they had not yet been found guilty of the offence alleged against them.

The dormitories were dingy and there seemed to be virtually no concern for hygiene and sanitation. The health of the children and their nutrition was quite clearly not a priority. There was no scope for any activity for the children either in terms of education or of any other nature for that matter. Most of the children would sit in front of a small TV and watch some programme or the other which did not seem to interest them. But they had no other option. Outside the building premises, but within the compound, there was a large garden, but that was out of bounds for the children. So, they could not play or exercise in the open. Their only option was to remain cooped up inside.

'On talking to some children, I was shocked to learn that a few had been in the Observation Home for more than five years although the maximum punishment that could be awarded under the law was only three years. Some of the children had spent several months in the Observation Home pending an enquiry for some petty offence alleged to have been committed. Privately, I believed that some of these children deserved to be on bail considering the pettiness of the alleged offence,' says Justice Lokur.

Towards the end of his visit, he requested the officials in the Home as well as the Board to review the case of each of these children within a week or two and let him know the result. After about two weeks, he went back to the Observation Home and was in for another shock. A review was conducted in the case of each child, as instructed, and it was found that 210 of them ought to have been released and were in fact released with the result that only forty-eight children now remained in the Home. It was quite obvious to him that until his visit nobody had cared for these children and perhaps some of them had even been forgotten about.

'This was my moment of truth, as it were, and I decided that something must be done to vastly improve the living conditions of children in the Observation Home and in all other Children's Homes in Delhi. I decided not to step back in making efforts to improve the life of children wherever they are and in whatever circumstances. It is because of these experiences that I have always encouraged persons who want to do something for children to visit the child care institutions so that they can see for themselves the condition in which the children are living. A visual impact is much more telling than reading about it,' said Justice Lokur.

Since then, Justice Madan Lokur has become one of the foremost champions of juvenile justice in the country. Whichever court he has served in—the High Courts of Assam, Andhra Pradesh and the Supreme Court of India—he has taken his passion and commitment to juvenile justice to them. As the first chairperson of the Juvenile Justice Committee of the Supreme Court of India, he has worked closely with the juvenile justice committees of the States, facilitated consultations at regional levels so that experiences and learning could be shared and performance reviewed. He has been single-handedly responsible for creating an interest in juvenile justice in the judiciary at different levels.

The first contact that children have with the justice system is the JJB. While it is true that a number of people who work in them treat their appointments as punishment postings, or sometimes even as easy postings, there are those that really wish to make a difference.

In a webinar on 28 June 2020,[6] Justice Rajiv Shakhder recounted how the Principal Magistrate in the case of the juvenile in the Nirbhaya case had come to them and shared how she wasn't convinced that the juvenile had been involved to the extent to which the media had reported it. The media was hounding the juvenile justice committee, of which he was a member, and the Principal Magistrate to reveal the date of the juvenile's release. In the interest of the child's safety, the committee advised her to advance the date of his release, thereby protecting him from public ire.

Spread across the country are many such young magistrates who put the letter and spirit of the law above their own prejudices or public and political pressure, sometimes at the peril of their own safety.

Justice Shakhder rightly called the media out for not doing their homework to find out the extent of the involvement of the juvenile. 'Juvenile justice is not rocket science. All it requires is compassion. If we were to only treat these children as we would treat our own, there would not be a problem,' he said.

One wonders if it is too much to ask of ourselves.

NOTES

Introduction

1 As per the Juvenile Justice (Care and Protection of Children) Act, 2015, Section 2(18), 'Child Welfare Police Officer' means an officer designated as such under sub-section (1) of Section 107, which states: 'In every police station, at least one officer, not below the rank of assistant sub-inspector, with aptitude, appropriate training and orientation may be designated as the child welfare police officer to exclusively deal with children either as victims or perpetrators, in co-ordination with the police, voluntary and non-governmental organizations.'

2 Nilashish Chaudhary, 'SC Accepts JK Juvenile Justice Committee's Findings Against Allegations Of Illegal Detention Of Children In Kashmir', Live Law, 13 December 2019 (https://www.livelaw.in/top-stories/sc-accepts-jk-juvenile-justice-committees-findings-that-no-children-are-illegally-detained-in-kashmir-150774, last accessed 21 November 2022).

3 'Satisfied with HC report saying no detention of minors in J&K: Supreme Court', Kashmir Life, 13 December 2019 (https://kashmirlife.net/satisfied-with-hc-report-saying-no-detention-of-minors-in-jk-supreme-court-220505, last accessed 21 November 2022).

4 Dr Subramanian Swamy and Ors vs Raju Thr. Member Juvenile Justice, Criminal Appeal No. 695 of 201 (Arising Out of SLP [Crl.] No. 1953 of 2013) (https://indiankanoon.org/doc/134314390/, last accessed 21 November 2022).

5 Kadra Pehadiya and Ors vs State of Bihar, AIR 1981 SC 939b; 1981 (29) BLJR 300; 1981 CriLJ 481; (1981) 3 SCC 671 (https://indiankanoon.org/doc/770248/, last accessed 21 November 2022).

6   As per the JJ Act, 2015, 'child in conflict with law' means a child who is alleged or found to have committed an offence and who has not completed eighteen years of age on the date of commission of such offence.

7   These are training sessions organized by diverse agencies: state judicial academies, NGOs, universities, police training academies/ schools, government departments, etc.

8   'Gurugram school murder: CBI chargesheets 16-yr-old, says accused googled ways to remove bloodstains, fingerprints', Firstpost, 5 February 2018 (https://www.firstpost.com/india/ryan-school-case-cbi-files-5000-page-chargesheet-against-class-xi-student-for-pradyuman-thakurs-murder-4336373.html, last accessed 21 November 2022).

9   '"He Sharpened Pencil, Put It In Too": Delhi Boy, 4, Assaults Classmate', NDTV, 24 November 2017 (https://www.ndtv.com/delhi-news/he-sharpened-pencil-put-it-in-too-delhi-boy-4-assaults-classmate-1779100, last accessed 21 November 2022).

10 'Delhi hit-and-run: Parents allowed teenager to drive without licence for 3 years', Hindustan Times, 26 March 2017 (https://www.hindustantimes.com/delhi/parents-allowed-teenager-to-drive-without-licence-for-three-years-says-chargesheet/story-k6iBIZNcP2gqFaCxqx9ouM.html, last accessed 21 November 2022).

11 '3 schoolboys arrested for girl's murder', The Times of India, 27 January 2003 (https://timesofindia.indiatimes.com/3-schoolboys-arrested-for-girls-murder/articleshow/35606045.cms, last accessed 21 November 2022).

12 'Lucknow boy kills mother for not letting him play online game, hides body for two days', The Indian Express, 9 June 2022 (https://indianexpress.com/article/cities/lucknow/lucknow-boy-kills-mother-pubg-hides-body-7958393/, last accessed 21 November 2022).

13 Kenneth B. Nunn, 'The Child as Other: Race and Differential Treatment in the Juvenile Justice System', DePaul Law Review, vol. 51, no. 679 (2001–02) (http://scholarship.law.ufl.edu/facultypub/108, last accessed 21 November 2022).

14 Stephen Wizner, 'The Child and the State: Adversaries in the Juvenile Justice System' (1972). Columbia Human Rights Law Review, vol. 4, no 389 (1972) (http://digitalcommons.law.yale.edu/fss_papers/1859, last accessed 21 November 2022).

1. Offender or Victim?

1 'Kimberly Jones—Speaking Out About Black Experiences in America | The Daily Social Distancing Show', YouTube (https://www.youtube.com/watch?v=U1k9APedIUY, last accessed 21 November 2022).

2 Each police district is under a Deputy Commissioner of *Police* (*DCP*).

3 G.S. Bajpai, Juvenile Justice: Impact and Implementation in India, Bloomsbury, 2019, p. 5.

4 Mohamed Huzaifa Javed Ahmed vs The State of Maharashtra, Criminal Appeal No. 1153 of 2018 (https://indiankanoon.org/doc/186425503/, last accessed 21 November 2022).

5 Juvenile in Conflict with the Law and Administration of Juvenile Justice System in States of Maharashtra and Rajasthan, Tata Institute of Social Sciences, Mumbai, 2016.

6 S.V. Ronad, A.S. Kori, S. Kosagi, P. Obanaik and P. Patil, 'Children in Conflict with Law in India', Nurse Care Open Access Journal, vol. 2, no. 3 (2017) (DOI: 10.15406/ncoaj.2017.02); Prakash Haveripet, 'Causes and Consequences of Juvenile Delinquency in India', Recent Research in Science and Technology, vol. 5, no. 3 (2013) (https://updatepublishing.com/journal/index.php/rrst/article/view/1038); and S. Sanyal, 'Reformation and Reintegration of Juveniles in Conflict with Law', Ministry of Women and Child Development, New Delhi, 2011.

7 B.S. Sharma and S. Dhillon, 'Juvenile Delinquency in India: A Cause for Concern', Journal of Indian Academy of Forensic Medicine, vol. 31, no. 1 (2009), pp. 68–70.

8 Saju Parackal and Rita Panicker, Children and Crime in India: Causes, Narratives and Interventions, Palgrave Macmillan, 2019, p. xiv.

9 Ibid., p. 3.

10 See Section 17 of the Report on Government Services 2020, Australian Government, Productivity Commission (https://www.pc.gov.au/research/ongoing/report-on-government-services/2020/community-services/youth-justice/rogs-2020-partf-section17.pdf, last accessed 21 November 2022).

11 'Repairing The Breach: A Brief History of Youth of Color in the Justice System', official website of the National Institute of Corrections, Department of Justice, United States Government (https://nicic.gov/

repairing-breach-brief-history-youth-color-justice-system-2015, last accessed 21 November 2022).

12 Nunn, 'The Child as Other: Race and Differential Treatment in the Juvenile Justice System'.

13 'It's Time to Close Youth Prisons', Vimeo (https://vimeo.com/445453514?fbclid=IwAR0NsF_ekFL3ZgTSVKd4XUFPKHi UMY8jJBbXmBJNR_HXb5Jou2GUvZZqoD0, last accessed 21 November 2022).

14 'A Majority of Voters Support an End to Extreme Sentences for Children', Fair and Just Prosecution, July 2020 (https://fairandjustprosecution.org/wp-content/uploads/2020/07/Juvenile-Life-Without-Parole-Polling-Report.pdf, last accessed 21 November 2022).

15 Buta Biberaj, Carol Siemon and Miriam Aroni Krinsky, 'Policymakers, Time to End Juvenile Life Sentencing', Juvenile Justice Information Exchange, 12 October 2020 (https://jjie.org/2020/10/12/policymakers-time-to-end-juvenile-life-sentencing/, last accessed 21 November 2022).

16 Ibid.

17 'Repairing The Breach'.

18 Ibid.

19 Jim Dwyer, 'The True Story of How a City in Fear Brutalized the Central Park Five', New York Times, 30 May 2019 (https://www.nytimes.com/2019/05/30/arts/television/when-they-see-us-real-story.html, last accessed 21 November 2022).

20 An 'observation home' is an institution established and maintained in every district or group of districts by a State government, either by itself, or through a voluntary or non-governmental organization, and is registered as such, for the purposes specified in sub-section (1) of Section 47 of the JJ Act, 2015. An OHB is an observation home for boys and an OHG is an observation home for girls.

21 As per the JJ Act, 2015 a 'special home' is 'an institution established by a State Government or by a voluntary or non-governmental organisation, registered under Section 48, for housing and providing rehabilitative services to children in conflict with the law, who are found, through inquiry, to have committed an offence and are sent to such institution by an order of the Board'. A 'place of safety' is 'any place or institution, not being a police lockup or jail, established

separately or attached to an observation home or a special home, as the case may be, the person in-charge of which is willing to receive and take care of the children alleged or found to be in conflict with law, by an order of the Board or the Children's Court, both during inquiry and ongoing rehabilitation after having been found guilty for a period and purpose as specified in the order'.

22 Ruzbeh N. Bharucha, My God is a Juvenile Delinquent, Sainathan Publications, p. 26.

23 Srivastava Divya, 'Understaffed and overcrowded, juvenile homes are hell holes rather than reform centres', Firstpost, 19 June 2016 (https://www.firstpost.com/living/understaffed-andovercrowded-juvenile-homes-are-hell-holes-rather-thanreform-centres-2842894.html, last accessed 21 November 2022).

24 Ibid., p. 25.

25 See 'Table 5A.5: Disposal of Juveniles Apprehended and Send to Courts (IPC & SLL) (State/UT-wise)–2021', Crime in India 2021, Vol. II, National Crime Records Bureau, Government of India (https://ncrb.gov.in/sites/default/files/CII-2021/CII_2021Volume%201.pdf, last accessed 21 November 2022).

26 See Article 1 of the United Nations Convention on the Rights of the Child.

27 Elizabeth S. Scott, Richard J. Bonnie and Laurence Steinberg, 'Young Adulthood as a Transitional Legal Category: Science, Social Change, and Justice Policy', Fordham Law Review, vol. 85, no. 641 (2016). Provided by Arthur W. Diamond Law Library, Columbia University Content, downloaded/printed from HeinOnline.

28 Penal Reform International (PRI), 'When the Crime Overshadows the Child: International standards and national practice in reconciling serious crime and childhood', 2014, UNICEF-India and PRI-UK.

29 Pat Thane, 'Childhood in History', in Barry Godson and John Muncie (eds), Youth Crime and Justice, Volume 1, Sage Library of Criminology, 2009.

30 Philippe Aries, Centuries of childhood, trans. Robert Baldick, London, 1973.

31 Anastasia Ulanowicz, 'Philippe Ariès', University of Pittsburg, n.d. (https://www.representingchildhood.pitt.edu/pdf/aries.pdf, last accessed 21 November 2022).

32 Susan M. Sawyer, 'The age of adolescence', The Lancet, vol. 2, no. 3 (March 2018) (https://www.thelancet.com/journals/lanchi/article/ PIIS2352-4642(18)30022-1/fulltext, last accessed 21 November 2022).

33 Richard J. Bonnie, Robert L. Johnson, Betty M. Chemers, and Julie A. Schuck, eds., 'Reforming Juvenile Justice: A Developmental Approach', for the Committee on Assessing Juvenile Justice Reform, Committee on Law and Justice, a Division of Behavioral and Social Sciences and Education, National Research Council, National Academies Press, Washington, DC, 2013, pp. 1–2.

34 PRI, 'When the Crime Overshadows the Child'.

2. The Anatomy of the Law

1 Donald P. Roper, Superintendent, Potosi Correctional Center, Petitioner vs Christopher Simmons, 543 US 551 (2005) (https://www. apa.org/about/offices/ogc/amicus/roper, last accessed 21 November 2022).

2 Austin Sarat, 'The Supreme Court is wrong. Even children who kill don't deserve life without parole', USA Today, 26 April 2021 (https:// www.usatoday.com/story/opinion/policing/2021/04/26/supreme- court-end-life-without-parole-children-column/7374361002/, last accessed 21 November 2022).

3 See Chapter XV. 363, Special Treatment of Child Offenders, Indian Jails Committee, 1919-1920.

4 See The Children Act, 1960, on the Ministry of Women and Child Development website (https://wcd.nic.in/children-act-1960-60-1960, last accessed 21 November 2022).

5 Ibid.

6 The Child Welfare Committees (CWC) are set up under the JJ Act in every district or for a group of districts for 'exercising the powers and to discharge the duties conferred on such Committees in relation to children in need of care and protection (CNCP) under this Act'. The CWC consists of a Chairperson, and four other members as the State government may think fit to appoint, of whom at least one shall be a woman and another, an expert on the matters concerning children. They together function as a bench of magistrates.

7 Sheela Barse & Ors vs Union of India & Ors, AIR 1986 SC 1773.

8　Ibid.

9　The competent authority, as per the new law, responsible for care, protection and rehabilitation of children in difficult circumstances; a bench of five persons.

10　The competent authority, as per the new law, responsible for adjudicating and disposing cases involving children in conflict with the law; a bench of three persons, headed by a judicial magistrate of first class and two social worker members.

11　See Sections 9 and 10 of the JJ Act.

12　Chapter I. Preliminary, The Juvenile Justice Act, 1986 (Act no. 53 of l986). It received the assent of the President on 1 December 1986 and was published in the Gazette of India on 3 December 1986.

13　'Child-Friendly Justice and Children's Rights', Official website of Child Rights International Network (CRIN), 2011 (https://archive.crin.org/en/library/publications/child-friendly-justice-and-childrens-rights.html, last accessed 21 November 2022).

14　Ibid.

15　India has States and Union Territories. Union Territories are directly under the Central government.

16　Available online http://www.indianlegislation.in/BA/BaActToc.aspx?actid=15585, last accessed 21 November 2022.

17　By 1986, when the first uniform legislation for delinquent children was passed in India, all States except Bihar had their own Children Act. Bihar was governed by the Children Ordinance, 1980.

18　United Nations Standard Minimum Rules for the Administration of Juvenile Justice ('The Beijing Rules'), adopted by the General Assembly resolution 40/33 of 29 November 1985. Parliament exercised its power under Article 253 of the Constitution read with Entry 14 of the Union List to make a law for the whole of India to fulfil international obligations. On 22 August 1986, the Juvenile Justice Bill, 1986 was introduced in the Lok Sabha.

19　'Juvenile Justice: Before and after the onset of Delinquency', working paper prepared by the Secretariat for the 6th UN Congress on the Prevention of Crime and the Treatment of Offenders, 9A/C0NF.87/5 (4 June 1980).

20　Chapter 1. Preliminary, The Juvenile Justice Act, 1986.

21　General Comment No. 24, replacing General Comment No. 10

(2007), Children's Rights in Juvenile Justice (https://www.ohchr.org/Documents/HRBodies/CRC/GC24/GeneralComment24.pdf, last accessed 21 November 2022).

3. The Stumbling Blocks

1   'December 16 gangrape juvenile accused to walk free in three years', The Indian Express, 1 September 2013 (http://archive.indianexpress.com/news/december-16-gangrape-juvenile-accused-to-walk-free-in-three-years/1162760/2, last accessed 21 November 2022).

2   'Nirbhaya case juvenile wasn't "most brutal"?', The Times of India, 3 October 2013 (http://timesofindia.indiatimes.com/city/delhi/Nirbhaya-case-juvenile-wasnt-most-brutal/articleshow/23426346.cms, last accessed 21 November 2022).

3   'An interview with Dr Ved Kumari', The Leaflet, 23 May 2018 (https://theleaflet.in/an-interview-with-dr-ved-kumari-on-her-latest-book-the-juvenile-justice-care-and-protection-of-children-act-2015-critical-analyses-and-the-state-of-juvenile-justice-in-india-in-t/, last accessed 21 November 2022).

4   'Maharashtra considers lowering juvenile age to 15 in heinous crime cases', Hindustan Times, 16 December 2017 (https://www.hindustantimes.com/mumbai-news/maharashtra-considers-lowering-juvenile-age-for-trial-in-heinous-crimes/story-hDsQw878WysK2mRtPOeBeJ.html, last accessed 21 November 2022).

5   'Why is early puberty a growing trend among Indian girls', Rediff.com, 7 July 2018 (rediff.com/getahead/report/health-why-is-early-puberty-a-growing-trend-among-indian-girls/20180707.htm#:~:text=Four%20years%20ago%2C%20a%20survey,earlier%20than%20in%20the%20past, last accessed 21 November 2022).

6   See the Wikipedia page for 'Age of criminal responsibility' (https://en.wikipedia.org/wiki/Defense_of_infancy, last accessed 21 November 2022).

7   Laurence Steinberg, 'Adolescent Brain Science and Juvenile Justice Policymaking', Psychology, Public Policy, and Law, vol. 23, no. 4 (2017), pp. 410–20 (http://dx.doi.org/10.1037/law0000128, last accessed 21 November 2022).

8   Elizabeth S. Scott et al., 'Young Adulthood as a Transitional Legal Category'.

9   Ibid.

10 See the UN Treaty Body Database (https://tbinternet.ohchr. org/_layouts/15/treatybodyexternal/Download.aspx?symbolno= CRC%2fC%2fGC%2f20&Lang=en, last accessed 21 November 2022).

11 Ibid. Article 41: 'Nothing in the present Convention shall affect any provisions which are more conducive to the realization of the rights of the child and which may be contained in: (a) The law of a State party; or (b) International law in force for that State.'

12 'An interview with Dr Ved Kumari'.

13 Ibid.

14 Ved Kumari, The Juvenile Justice (Care and Protection of Children) Act 2015. Critical Analysis, Universal Law Publishers, 2017.

15 Ibid.

16 Arul Verma, 'Unshrouding the Enigma Behind Preliminary Assessment Under the Juvenile Justice (Care And Protection Of Children) Act, 2015', Journal of the Indian Law Institute, vol. 62, no 3 (2020).

17 For example, see Leena Dhangkhar, 'Juvenile justice board in Gurugram has tried 38 juveniles as adults since January 2016', Hindustan Times, 22 May 2018 (https://www.hindustantimes.com/gurugram/juvenile-justice-board-in-gurugram-has-tried-38-juveniles-as-adults-since-january-2016/story-SSNEIcjgeMf5V9W0YPgMnO.html, last accessed 21 November 2022).

18 'New Juvenile Justice Act: Two teenagers sentenced to life imprisonment for murder', Firstpost, 1 March 2017 (https://www.firstpost.com/india/new-juvenile-justice-act-two-teenagers-sentenced-to-life-imprisonment-for-murder-3308528.html, last accessed 21 November 2022).

19 'Hyderabad: 19-yr-old who sodomised, killed a boy when he was minor gets lifer', The Times of India, 28 June 2019 (https://timesofindia. indiatimes.com/city/hyderabad/19-yr-old-who-sodomised-killed-a-boy-when-he-was-minor-gets-lifer/articleshow/69981332.cms, last accessed 21 November 2022).

20 Salil Mekaad, 'Tried as adults, minors sentenced to life term for murder by Jhabua court', The Times of India, 1 March 2017 (https://

timesofindia.indiatimes.com/city/indore/tried-as-adults-minors-sentenced-to-life-for-murder-by-jhabua-court/articleshow/57410446.cms, last accessed 29 November 2022).

21 'Explained: When a juvenile is tried as an adult, when not', The Indian Express, 22 July 2019 (https://indianexpress.com/article/explained/when-a-juvenile-is-tried-as-an-adult-when-not-5840823/, last accessed 21 November 2022).

22 HJA vs The State of Maharashtra, Criminal Appeal No. 1153 of 2018 (https://indiankanoon.org/doc/186425503/, last accessed 21 November 2022).

23 Ved Kumari, The Juvenile Justice Act.

24 Mohamed Huzaifa Javed Ahmed vs The State of Maharashtra.

25 Shilpa Mittal vs State of NCT of Delhi & Anr, Criminal Appeal No. 34 of 2020.

26 Mumtaz Ahmed Nasir Khan vs State of Maharashtra and Ors, Criminal Appeal No. 1153 of 2018.

27 Durga Meena vs State of Rajasthan, Criminal Appeal No. 27 of 2019.

28 Bail Matters No. 2220/2021, State versus Nikhil Kumar @ Chohi, FIR No. 915/2020, PS Bindapur, U/s 323/326/341/302/34 IPC (https://images.assettype.com/barandbench/2021-07/6b0374f1-026b-4f11-849c-f682b06de79c/State_v_Nikhil_Kumar.pdf, last accessed 21 November 2022).

29 Court on its Own Motion vs Dept of Women and Child, WP(C) No. 8889 of 2011 (https://indiankanoon.org/doc/132059140/, last accessed 21 November 2022).

30 'Over 123 Juveniles in Tihar: Why Children End Up in "Adult Jails"', The Quint, 27 July 2021 (https://www.thequint.com/news/law/how-delhi-incarcerates-juveniles-in-adult-prisons, last accessed 21 November 2022).

31 Ibid.

32 Ibid.

33 Personal communication with the author.

34 The JJ Act requires an individual care plan of the child entering the juvenile justice system to ensure the process of rehabilitation and social integration of children under this Act and therefore the need for such a plan has been reiterated in the Act at several places. Form 7 in the JJ Rules provides a format that is to be used to prepare this plan.

35 Personal communication with the author. Since the person is still a member of the JJB, their identity is not revealed.

36 Personal communication with the author.

37 Under the JJ Act a 'child care institution' (CCI) means any facility that houses children—a children's home, open shelter, observation home, special home, place of safety, or a specialized adoption agency—and a fit facility recognized under this Act for providing care and protection to children who are in need of such services.

38 Personal communication with the author.

39 Special Juvenile Police Units.

40 HJA vs The State of Maharashtra.

41 'Juvenile Justice', youth.gov (https://youth.gov/youth-topics/juvenile-justice, last accessed 21 November 2022).

4. The Children Who 'Offend'

1 'Over 123 Juveniles in Tihar', The Quint, 27 July 2021.

2 'Nirbhaya case juvenile wasn't "most brutal"?', The Times of India, 3 October 2013.

3 A debate on the news channel Mirror Now which I participated in.

4 Richard J. Bonnie et al., 'Reforming Juvenile Justice: A Developmental Approach'.

5 Ibid.

6 PRI, 'When the Crime Overshadows the Child'.

7 Chirag had been referred to the Delhi-based child rights organization Leher, who have shared this case with the author for inclusion in this book.

8 Section 83 of the IPC says that '[n]othing is an offence which is done by a child above seven years of age and under twelve, who has not attained sufficient maturity of understanding to judge of the nature and consequences of his conduct on that occasion'.

9 See, for example, the study by B.S. Sharma and S. Dhillon, 'Juvenile Delinquency in India: A Cause for Concern'.

10 Malvika Tyagi, 'Understanding Juvenile Crime: Notes from the Field', Economic & Political Weekly, vol. 51, no. 2 (9 January 2016).

11 Richa Arora, 'A Study on Children In Conflict with Law, A Delhi Based Study', Centre for Equity and Justice for Children and Families,

School of Social Work, Tata Institute of Social Sciences, Mumbai, 2017.

12 Durga Meena vs State of Rajasthan.

13 Charged under Section 304A of IPC—Causing death by negligence: 'Whoever causes the death of any person by doing any rash or negligent act not amounting to culpable homicide, shall be punished with imprisonment of either description for a term which may extend to two years, or with fine, or with both.'

14 'Delhi teen who ran over exec with dad's car won't be tried as adult: Supreme Court', Hindustan Times, 10 January 2020 (https://www.hindustantimes.com/delhi-news/delhi-teen-who-ran-over-exec-with-dad-s-car-won-t-be-tried-as-adult-supreme-court/story-3KwunJ6jGkVMGah5aHJAfM.html, last accessed 21 November 2022).

15 'Greater Noida twin murder: Teen confesses to killing mother and sister, was upset after being scolded', Hindustan Times, 10 December 2017 (https://www.hindustantimes.com/noida/scolding-led-to-killing-noida-teenager-confesses-to-murder-of-mother-sister/story-5jgYkjWWC9YOpMNrFx7Y8J.html, last accessed 21 November 2022).

16 'Ryan International case: Killed Pradyuman to avoid exams, parent-teacher meeting, says Class 11 boy', Zee News, 8 November 2017 (https://zeenews.india.com/india/ryan-international-case-killed-pradyuman-thakur-to-avoid-exams-parent-teacher-meeting-class-11-boy-tells-cbi-2055255.html, last accessed 21 November 2022).

17 'Ryan school murder: One brutal killing, multiple theories and wait for justice', Hindustan Times, 18 November 2017 (https://www.hindustantimes.com/gurgaon/ryan-school-murder-police-blamed-conductor-cbi-says-class-11-student-but-who-killed-pradhyumn/story-HZeYf4G70Rs0iSUbsWWsuK.html, last accessed 21 November 2022); and 'Ryan International School murder case: Class 11 boy accused of murdering junior was a "bully", say classmates', Firstpost, 9 November 2017 (https://www.firstpost.com/india/ryan-international-school-murder-case-class-xi-boy-accused-of-murdering-pradyuman-was-a-bully-say-classmates-4200807.html, last accessed 21 November 2022).

18 'Pradyuman murder: Detained Ryan student a porn addict, often carried knife to school', India Today, 9 November 2017 (https://

www.indiatoday.in/mail-today/story/pradyuman-thakur-murder-ryan-international-school-detained-student-porn-addict-gurugram-cbi-1082463-2017-11-09, last accessed 21 November 2022).

19   'Supreme Court Grants Interim Bail To Accused Who Was Juvenile At The Time Of Crime', Live Law, 20 October 2022 (https://www.livelaw.in/top-stories/ryan-school-murder-case-supreme-court-grants-interim-bail-to-accused-who-was-juvenile-at-the-time-of-crime-212171, last accessed 21 November 2022).

20   'Boy murders two to fulfil dream of becoming a dancer', Hindustan Times, 21 March 2016 (https://www.hindustantimes.com/delhi/boy-murders-two-to-fulfil-dream-of-becoming-a-dancer/story-jUI1l6iQhgnljqKGtd7AKN.html, last accessed 21 November 2022).

21   'One in seven persons in India suffers from mental disorders: ICMR study', Business Standard, 23 December 2019 (https://www.business-standard.com/article/news-ani/one-in-seven-persons-in-india-suffers-from-mental-disorders-icmr-study-119122300546_1.html#:~:text=The%20research%20has%20shown%20that,dis,   last accessed 21 November 2022).

22   'Father of Class 12 boy who jumped to death blames girl's online post', The Times of India, 8 May 2020 (https://timesofindia.indiatimes.com/city/gurgaon/father-of-class-12-boy-who-jumped-to-death-blames-girls-online-post/articleshow/75614072.cms, last accessed 21 November 2022).

23   'Young Children Being Radicalised, Need to Identify & Put Them in De-radicalisation Camps: Bipin Rawat', News 18, 17 January 2020 (https://www.news18.com/news/india/young-children-being-radicalised-need-to-identify-and-put-them-in-de-radicalisation-camps-says-bipin-rawat-2459711.html, last accessed 21 November 2022).

5. Those Who Never Give Up on Children

1   Ved Kumari, 'Construction of Criminality and Children', Essex Human Rights Review—UKIERI Special Issue: Realising Children's Rights: Multidisciplinary, Comparative and Practical Perspectives, December 2010.

2   'An interview with Dr Ved Kumari'.

3   A juvenile may be sent temporarily to a place of safety, or an observation home during the pendency of an enquiry before the competent authority. Sections 16(7), 21(1)(b) and (c) and 33, JJ Act, 1986.

4   Personal communication with the author.

5   Personal communication with the author.

6   'Historical Evolution of Juvenile Justice Committee (JJC) in India', YouTube (https://www.youtube.com/watch?v=PsXdI5yUer8, last accessed 21 November 2022).

PART TWO

MOVING ON

Kalpana Purushothaman

I believe the juvenile justice system can be that door that
lets the future in for children in conflict with the law.

—Graham Greene,
The Power and the Glory

I was working with a community-based initiative in a
slum in Adugodi, Bangalore at that time. As part of this
initiative we worked with children and young adults,
providing them with counselling support and life skills. I
knew nothing about juvenile justice. I had no idea that
there were laws that were meant for children who may have
committed crimes. I did, however, know that many of the
children that I worked with were on drugs and sometimes
'got into trouble with the cops' for getting involved in petty
thefts and fights.

Manish was one such boy who often came for our
programmes. One day, Manish's mother came looking for
me saying her son had been picked up by the police. She
said, 'Akka, can you come with me to the station? They are
refusing to let him go. You speak English, the police will
listen to you.'

Fifteen-year-old Manish had been taken by the police for questioning, allegedly with regard to the theft of a bicycle. Manish had not returned for a week and despite repeated visits to the police station, his mother was not allowed to meet him, nor were the police forthcoming with any information on his whereabouts. They rudely sent the mother packing every time she approached them. And thus she had sought my help.

When I went to the police station with the mother, we were told that after some basic enquiries, Manish had been released the very same day that he was picked up. But it had been over a week and Manish had not come home yet. I asked the policeman if he had any information about where Manish might have gone, given that he had not returned home. The policeman countered with a question of his own, 'Are you a lawyer?' When I replied in the negative, he warned me angrily to mind my own business and not cause further trouble. Upset, insulted and afraid, Manish's mother and I went back, hoping that wherever he had gone, he would come home soon.

A week later, Manish turned up in a ditch near my workplace—dead.

My journey in this field started with Manish. His death taught me some valuable lessons—being poor and marginalized in India meant that you could be suspected of being involved in any crime in your locality, whether you actually had anything to do with it or not. It brought home very quickly the stark reality that being poor was already a crime—that the police would not answer your questions, that the media would not be interested in your story and the nation would not want to know about your fight for a fair hearing, never mind actual justice.

This was my harsh introduction to children in conflict with the law, the 'system' and what can happen to them.

Manish affected me deeply and I wanted to know more about this system and how it worked. So, two years later, armed with a post-graduate degree in Child Rights Law from the National Law School India University (NLSIU), Bangalore and backed by my education and experience of psychology, I set out to be a counsellor for children in conflict with the law at the Observation Home, Madivala, Bangalore. While I was familiar with working with children and counselling, I had little exposure to the juvenile justice system that I was about to enter. Nothing could have prepared me. No degree or experience could have helped me make sense of the soul-shattering experiences in the Observation Home in Bangalore, right in the middle of one of the most bustling and lively vegetable markets in the city.

For the next few years, I worked as a senior counsellor and researcher as part of the Juvenile Justice Programme, Centre for Child and the Law, NLSIU. I had the privilege of learning from the hundreds of children I interacted with through my work—children with neither privilege nor resources.

Over the years, numerous children and families have generously shared their stories and their lives with me. As we stumbled through our shared journey through the juvenile justice system, I realized how easily vulnerable children from poor and troubled homes got lured into crime—sometimes with just the promise of biryani and/or 'ganja'. I saw how local dons recruited and groomed impressionable boys from broken families into a world of crime. I learnt with utter shock and dismay that almost all children in the Observation Home (OH) were from poor or marginalized backgrounds.

Very rarely did I come across any child from a middle-class or affluent background. Yes, they came in too—but only if there was media coverage or it was a sensational case. They had a safety net, something that children from marginalized families did not have at all.

This was also the period in my life when I struggled with how to answer my former colleagues who would ask me about 'job satisfaction'—in my work with 'budding criminals', as one of my friends sarcastically put it. Of course, I would give them the expected (and often truthful) answer of being overworked and underpaid. A chronic sense of fatigue and burn-out had become part of my life, which is probably familiar to all those working with child rights issues.

But I had found a sense of purpose and enjoyed the work I was doing.

What kept me going all these years were the amazing children who loved me so generously, challenged all my notions of counselling and held me through some of the toughest years of my personal and professional life. The astounding resilience of these children is mind-boggling to me even today.

Having said that, there were many struggles and challenges too. This work presents one with some 'events' which, I suppose, one cannot really leave behind or move on from. I haven't healed from them but have soldiered on.

I have been repeatedly told by my therapist, my friends and some colleagues at work that I must learn to move on from the often relentless and unending trauma and tragedy that one encounters on an almost daily basis in this field of work. I promise you, I have tried. But how do you really move on from watching a child you knew die a sudden, violent death? How do you move on when you bury a boy you hoped to heal?

That is the story of Vishnu. He was around 19 or 20 years old when he was hacked to death at a traffic signal on Bangalore's famous MG Road. I was one of the people he had spoken to in the last twenty-four hours of his life. He had been so excited and had called to share with me that he was taking up a job as a driver in a travel company. He wanted to take me out for a 'treat', but I was out of Bangalore. So, we fixed up to meet up over the weekend. I was so happy. This was yet another 'success case' where a CICL had found his way back into the 'mainstream'. Isn't that what we were working for?

I had first met Vishnu at the OH when he was 15–16 years old. He was assigned to me for counselling by the Juvenile Justice Board. Vishnu and his two friends had stolen a manhole cover and sold it for Rs 3,000. They were apprehended and were placed in the OH.

Vishnu spent about six months in the Home. There he met children who were 'smarter' than him, who were there for drug-related crimes and were addicts. But he promised me that he was not one of them. He told me he was keen to study. I believed him and arranged for tuition classes with a local volunteer. He did not let me down and passed his class 10 Board exam through the National Open School system. He had his struggles with drugs which he had learnt to use during his time at the OH, but he was coping with it. His uncle, who was a driver, taught him how to drive and he was soon going to apply for his license and take up that job at the travel company. That is when he had called me.

When Vishnu was killed, I was distraught. I blamed myself. I went over every detail of my conversations with him and his mother over and over again.

After being released on bail and leaving the OH, Vishnu

had returned home. His mother often complained and scolded him about his addiction. She complained to me too, that's how I knew. Unfortunately, he was now out of the system. Since the JJB's orders regarding his counselling did not extend beyond the time he was in the OH, I had no 'legal authority' to call him or to question him. I could do so informally and I tried. Like all teenagers he laughed it off and said he did smoke beedis occasionally, but that his mother was over-reacting. I told him to be careful and left it at that. Was I wrong to have done that? Should I have confronted him? These are questions that haunt me still.

A few hours after his last call to me, Vishnu was murdered in cold blood, the act captured on the CCTV camera of the traffic signal. I found out when, a day later, I got a call from the father of another child, Jaggu, who told me that the police had picked up his son for investigation into Vishnu's death. I froze and hoped that the information was wrong.

But a few hours later, as I stood at Victoria Hospital with Vishnu's body tightly wrapped in bandages smelling of blood, urine and some unknown chemicals, I was forced to confront the truth. We took Vishnu home.

Rathna, Vishnu's mother collapsed and fell heavily against me as I struggled to stay calm amidst the uproar in the crowded alley in front of Vishnu's house. Someone gave us a bench to place his body on while someone else brought out a sheet and covered him. Within minutes, an oil lamp, flowers and incense appeared and people emerged from their houses, some of them standing silently around while some were weeping openly.

A local municipal leader mobilized people from the neighbourhood to help bury Vishnu in an open space nearby. He told me they would plant a tree at the spot as it was a local belief that the spirit of the dead child would bloom and blossom and comfort his family and the community that he was still amidst them. Never had I felt more gratitude for these ancient beliefs.

As I was called upon to put in the first handful of mud and initiate the rituals for burial, someone asked who I was. Rathna looked at the person and answered, she is his mother. I thought I had heard wrongly, and looked at her. She looked straight at me and said, 'She is the mother he spoke to last before dying, I am the mother who fed him his last meal.' In that hour of grief, that generous mother shared her child with me in a way that I can never really be thankful enough for. Or understand why.

And that is why I find I cannot move on. Especially from the death of a child I had once cared for.

But Vishnu taught me many important personal and professional lessons. As a counsellor, we have to deal with hundreds of children in diverse situations of distress and adversity. It is important that even as we empathize with the children and their situation, we also learn to keep a healthy professional distance.

Being a counsellor for CICLs has taught me how inadequate our education, training and professional experiences often are. Vishnu taught me that 'countertransference' can happen and haunt a therapist later in life. 'Post-traumatic stress' happens to counsellors too, not just clients.

I knew that what I suffered from after his death was just that—nightmares with vivid flashbacks of Vishnu being hacked as he sat on a motorbike at the signal. I continued to get 'triggered' into a panic attack by all kinds of strange things or situations, ranging from traffic signals to 'hospital smells'. These panic attacks were the new normal for me for a long time. Rathna and I stayed in touch and spoke over the phone for hours going over his last phone call, his last meal, his memories, over and over again. She met me several times and I went to her home where she showed me his clothes, his pictures, his possessions—all carefully preserved. I was no longer the counsellor. We were just two mothers sharing the common grief of losing a child.

No, I did not and could not move on. I am not sure I still have. But after so many years and so many children I have worked with in the justice system, I have come to firmly believe that there is always hope for children who offend—but only if each child can be given the support he or she needs. Sometimes we can and sometimes, despite our best intentions, we cannot. But I am convinced we must try. With all the competence and compassion we can summon within ourselves.

Boundary Crossings and Boundary Violations

When I first met Rani, she was a scared 15-year-old girl. She had gone through months of multiple and repeated sexual assault inside a brothel where she had been beaten, drugged, and forced into commercial sex work. She had come into the juvenile justice system charged under the Immoral Trafficking Prevention Act, 1956 (ITPA) for having lured another child into sex work.

Rani's preferred mode of ensuring she was brought in for therapy was to cut herself. Her biological mother had committed suicide when Rani was 6 years old. For some reason, after a few sessions, she began calling me 'Amma' no matter what I told her. She told everyone at the State Reception Home for Women where she was being held, that

I was her mother and that she would complain about them to me if they bullied her.

Rani was a good-looking girl with expressive eyes, but none of that was visible in those early days immediately after her apprehension by the police, because all one could see was tangled hair which she refused to comb, layers of dirt streaking her face, and a foul smell as she neither brushed her teeth nor washed herself.

So for months after our initial meeting, we worked on 'counselling' goals of basic hygiene and self-care. Each session ending with her promising to bathe, brush her teeth, comb her hair and not cut herself till we met again. Given her situation, I met her once or twice a week at the time. Each time we discovered that we could not meet our 'counselling goals'—till one evening when she told me that she liked the perfume I was wearing. So, we 'revised' our goals to now mention that if she kept her side of the bargain, I would 'maybe' consider some cosmetics for her. Next week, she came in with a washed face and asked for powder and soap. Meeting our 'hygiene goals' were a breeze after that. Every subsequent session, she turned up with new progress. We went from washing the face, to brushing teeth daily, to washing hair weekly, and then to bathing twice or thrice a week. All in less than two months. I kept my promise and got her a perfume. Four months later, for her sixteenth birthday, I bought her what she called 'fancy bra', perfume and some new clothes. My fellow partner in crime, Rani's child psychiatrist put together a 'gift hamper' with shampoos, a moisturizer, face cream and lip gloss. Rani hugged me and squealed with joy when she opened her 'gift packet'. For the first time in months, she cried.

Many survivors of sexual abuse—both children and

adults—often suffer from a poor body image and find it difficult to accept their bodies, often blaming their looks or their attractiveness for the abuse they had to suffer. Many child and teen survivors who were treated as sexual objects by their abusers hide behind baggy clothes, unwashed bodies and poor hygiene in a desperate attempt that perhaps now no one will find them attractive enough to sexually abuse them again. Rani's taking care of her body, wearing makeup, and taking interest in looking good again was a huge milestone in her process of learning to love herself again and thinking herself worthy of being loved.

Rani left the institution about three years later and moved on. But I found that I needed to continue to work with this child, now a grown woman of 23 years. But I have not forgotten that moment of pure joy when she held her hamper. The total vulnerability when she wept holding me softly, whispering, 'Thank you, Amma.'

I was taught in my professional training that I must never violate therapeutic boundaries—especially those that involved giving gifts to patients and clients. Was Rani my patient/client? Well, technically and professionally, I was her counsellor, so yes. But was there only a technical and professional relationship between us? Didn't she and I heal wounds—sometimes hers and sometimes mine—together? Didn't she teach me and inspire me as much as I held her and showed her what mothering could sometimes look like? What if we did away with the power equation in these therapist-client relationships that frame one as the expert and the other as a victim—somehow lesser? After all, she was and is the expert on her life, not me. What if we could reach out to each other in the spirit of humanity and universal sisterhood? As human beings, as co-travellers in the human journey. These are questions that constantly come to me.

Rani taught me that therapy sometimes looks dangerously similar to parenting—an exhausting, thankless and never-ending job. I held Rani through two boyfriends and three jobs, a runaway marriage to an illegal immigrant with whom she went to Assam, name change and conversion to Islam, domestic violence in her marital relationship, an abortion at a remote primary health centre in Silchar and much more that I have forgotten now. Through it all, Rani remained a lovely and resilient young woman, teaching herself cooking, embroidery, tailoring and enrolling in local self-help groups that taught her to save money.

Three years after her marriage, in 2018, she returned to Bangalore with her husband, found a job at a garment factory supporting herself and her husband and occasionally even sending a few thousand rupees to her father. In December 2019, her husband wiped out her life savings of Rs 70,000 and fled to Assam as his family's name was not mentioned in the NRC (National Register of Citizens) list.

Heartbroken and bankrupt, Rani now lives alone in Bangalore, with no documents that she can use to prove her identity—either before marriage or after marriage. She does not want to use her earlier name as it reminds her of her earlier life and time as a 'child in conflict with the law'. Her husband has taken their marriage certificate and her Aadhaar card, which she is convinced will be used for someone else in his family.

Her life is completely conflicted. She now hates her new name and religion, which she had embraced for love. She now associates it with her husband who she feels has cheated and abandoned her. The police from her neighbourhood, who are aware of her past, periodically turn up at her home and her father's home to demand money saying they can arrest her anytime now on charges of prostitution if she refuses to pay.

Living alone, she has not told anyone at work or in her neighbourhood that her husband has abandoned her as she is afraid of being sexually attacked if it is known that she is a single woman. She has quietly moved in with a female colleague at work.

And yet there is no escape. She is now being blackmailed by one of her husband's friends. He is threatening to tell her employers and her landlord that she was once a commercial sex worker and a child in conflict with the law and ensure that she has no job and no roof over her head. In return he is demanding money and sexual favours from her.

Despite all the theory of the 'principle of fresh start' and anonymity of the child in conflict with the law under the JJ Act, the fact is that children who offend are seldom able to get rid of the stigma. It is double jeopardy if it's a girl.

As for me, I keep asking myself: What boundaries of profession, relationship and humanity must I cross again to ensure Rani gets a decent shot at life?

Missing the Wood for the Trees

Karthik was 15 years old and in the ninth standard when I first met him. He had been charged with brutal sexual assault on a 4-year-old girl called Sonia from his school. On his second day at the OH, he told me he was ashamed that he had brought shame to his grandfather, who was a much-respected school teacher in a nearby village. On day five, I met him again, when he told me that actually it wasn't him who had assaulted Sonia but that another boy named Dileep, the son of a police Sub-Inspector, had done it and put the blame on him. He further shared that Dileep used to watch porn videos which he shared with Karthik from time to time on his phone.

Alarmed and worried that Karthik might be getting framed for what someone else had done, I immediately set about finding out more. Along with his lawyer (also a colleague of mine), I went to the scene of the crime, met his teachers, neighbours and found that there was no Dileep—in his class or in the entire school. Nor did any SI's son study in the entire school. But having learnt our lessons in child rights that ingrain in us the expression 'believe the child', we do just that. I did not believe the school or the neighbours and kept looking for Dileep. I was not being gullible or naive. I was only doing what I had been trained to do.

Three weeks later, Karthik got bail. When I met him next, he kept to his version that he had not assaulted the girl. His father was with him. According to Karthik's father, his son was being framed by the girl's family because of a dispute between them over some financial matter. But what about the medical reports of Sonia—a fractured nose, a forehead smashed with a stone, lip which was cut and severe injuries to her private parts? Didn't it clearly show that sexual assault had taken place? And what about Dileep and his father? More importantly, what about the porn videos found in Karthik's phone?

'I don't know about that,' Karthik's father told me flatly, 'but my son is being framed.' Something did not feel right. I was not so convinced this time.

I was Karthik's counsellor, and along with the NIMHANS (National Institute of Mental Health and Neurosciences) team at Bangalore, we worked for over a year with Karthik, his father, mother and grandfather. I felt that he came close to disclosure many times, always stopping short of a full confession, but leaving me with many dangling clues and cues. He would describe (rather accurately corroborated by the police report) what Sonia was wearing on the day of the sexual assault and then suddenly stop and say, 'But you know, that day I didn't really meet her.' Or he would disclose in great detail about the sexual abuse that he had undergone as a 10-year-old by a lady teacher in his previous school. He would say that he felt really angry about his abuse and often thought that he must take 'revenge' by sexually assaulting someone else—and then stop short if I asked him if he had actually tried to do so.

And then almost a year later, one night I got a call from Karthik's mother, Shanthi, which was a bolt from the blue. Shanthi was a very quiet woman who always looked worried and afraid and sat silently through all sessions. She would nervously answer any questions put to her in a few syllables and again lapse into silence. Karthik's father never let her or Karthik out of his sight and always insisted on accompanying them to every therapy session. That night on the phone, Shanthi told me what I had failed to find out in so many months. She told me that her husband had been sexually abusing Karthik since he was 3–4 years old, and that he still did that. If she protested, she was beaten and silenced. He insisted on bathing his 16-year-old son himself every day and checked every part of his body. He physically and violently disciplined Karthik who was terrified of his father. She told me that she not only believed but knew that Karthik was guilty of raping Sonia and that the only way of saving her son would be for the JJB to find him guilty and send him to a Special Home for rehabilitation and treatment. She begged me to tell the JJB that her son was guilty but not that she had revealed it.

In one of my toughest ethical dilemmas, I decided confidentiality was more important than disclosure, that my role as a counsellor was to help the child and his family heal. My role as a counsellor was not that of criminal investigation into guilt or innocence. I did not tell the JJB about his mother's disclosure and waited for the Board to arrive at their own conclusions. Since the child had 'technically' not admitted his guilt, his lawyer decided to plead 'not guilty'.

I am not alone in this professional predicament. Many counsellors working with children in the justice system are faced with this dilemma. We are meant to 'counsel and heal' the children. What children say to us is supposed to be privileged information. Children often openly share what they have done in the belief that they won't be judged by us and that their secrets are safe with us. As counsellors, we are probably the first human beings in their lives who accept them as they are and it is this acceptance that forms the foundation for them to trust others in the justice system. Counsellors can assist and support the child to make a disclosure to the Board, if they so wish. But should we be sharing privileged information as evidence? I don't believe so. My belief is that investigation into guilt is the work of the Board. The mental health professional, whether a counsellor, psychologist or psychiatrist is there to give support by providing details of the social, medical, psychological and other life circumstances of the child that enable the Board to understand the circumstances which made the child come into conflict with the law and the steps that must be taken to enable rehabilitation and social reintegration of the child.

Shanthi's phone call taught me an invaluable lesson that

night. All my training and experience as a counsellor failed me as I had simply overlooked the possibility of sexual abuse by the father! I had been totally blind and misread his involvement in his son's life as parental concern. I had skipped the basic standard procedure of ruling out sexual abuse by other adults in the child's life—even though the child had disclosed sexual abuse by an adult (the lady teacher). I now wondered if she was real and whether all along Karthik had been trying to give me clues that would lead me to discover the abuse by his father. I wondered if Dileep was real or a figment of Karthik's imagination, or just a childish attempt by a wounded child to protect his father even as he desperately tried to reach out for help for himself.

In fighting for Karthik's right to health and rehabilitation, I had neglected to pay attention to other realities which were just as important. The reality of the harm caused to the victim and her family. The reality that no one, including parents, siblings, spouse could be assumed to be not guilty of having harmed the child sitting before me. I had forgotten that power—of being a parent, in this case—can sometimes be as corrupting and damaging for a child as any other.

Karthik was found guilty and sentenced to six months at the Special Home, despite my Individual Care Plan (ICP) recommending a three-year-long intensive rehabilitation plan including psychiatric treatment. I truly believed that that was what was in his best interest. Karthik's parents refused to speak to me as I explained the ICP to them. Shanthi though looked at me and smiled faintly for the first time in eighteen months.

As the final order pronouncing him 'guilty' was read to him at the JJB, Karthik had a blackout and passed out cold right outside the room. I rushed him to NIMHANS where he was advised admission and in-patient treatment. Even as I watched helplessly, his father got him discharged at 11.00 pm the same night, against medical advice, and took him home. A few days later, he was placed at the Special Home, but his father had already filed an appeal against the JJB order, in the sessions court, which granted him bail. So he took his son home. That was the last we saw or heard of Karthik. He and his family vanished without a trace. I am not sure whether the police are even looking for them.

If this case had happened today, I would have been forced to report Karthik's sexual abuse as reporting is now mandatory. This was in 2011 before the Protection of Children from Sexual Offences Act, 2012 had been passed and hence mandatory reporting was not in force then. At that time, I was caught in the dilemma placed before me by Karthik's mother. She had begged me not to tell anyone. Reporting the sexual abuse of Karthik by his father would have meant that I would have also had to report her as the source of the information, since Karthik had not revealed anything.

I often think about what might have happened to Karthik. Where might he be today? In school or college? In jail? In a hospital somewhere? Did he find a good friend, confidante or counsellor with whom he could share his troubled secrets and find some solace? Were there more victims or did he make a clean break from his past? Did he grow up to have the courage to confront his father? Did he take his 'revenge' after all?

Tough Love

Once in a while there comes along a child who I must *learn* to love. A child who will make it really difficult for me to reach out to and want to help. An often raging, violent, troubled child who will put me in touch with my own anger and unkindness. These are the children I know I must make the effort to love.

Umesh was around 15–16 years old when I first met him. It was 2017, and by then, I had moved from being a counsellor to a member of the Juvenile Justice Board, Bangalore (Urban). Bright and full of beans, Umesh simply wouldn't sit still in one place. He loved to talk and would talk nineteen to the dozen the minute he spotted me anywhere at the OH. His father was a chronic alcoholic who regularly and violently abused Umesh, his mother, Meena, and his younger brother, Mahesh. When Umesh was around 11–12 years old, his father took an iron rod and hit Umesh, splitting his head open. Meena rushed him to NIMHANS and Umesh was saved just in time, but with several stitches down the back of his head that he loved to show off to anyone who cared to listen. That incident was probably the last straw that broke the camel's back. Meena walked out with her two children and started living on her own. Umesh felt that he was now the 'man of the house' and that he must now take care of his mother and younger brother. He tried doing odd jobs and earned a bit of money but it was never quite enough. An older colleague at the garage where he worked taught him to steal and sell some motor parts for money. Which is when he was apprehended for the first time. Out on bail, another older colleague took him along on a ride and stole a motorbike. Umesh was apprehended again but he had now graduated to serious crime. A year later, Mahesh also dropped out of school and joined Umesh in his illegal activities and landed up at the OH just as often as Umesh. Meena's entire life revolved around getting both her boys out on bail and keeping them away from the police who would drop in at odd hours looking for them.

While he was out on bail, Umesh got involved with a group of adults who took him along for a robbery and he landed up at Parapannagrahara—the central prison in Bangalore. It was here that Umesh first met Sudesh.

Sudesh was almost 18 and had several cases against him, the most serious of them being attempt to murder and robbery. Sudesh had been working at a bakery in Odisha for almost a year as a child labourer when he felt that he could start off on his own back home in Karnataka. He stole about a lakh rupees from his employer and headed home. When his mother and brother-in-law scolded him about this, he got angry and violently attacked his brother-in-law. His mother threw him out of home and he went to stay with a friend. This friend was into drugs and part of a gang that was involved in petty theft in the locality. Sudesh was arrested and taken to Parapannagrahara along with three other gang members for attempting to break into a locked house.

Umesh's lawyer who had represented him for the other case before the JJB, offered to represent Sudesh as well, and presenting documents that showed that both were juveniles and not adults, got them transferred to the OH, Bangalore. But before that happened, both Umesh and Sudesh had already spent seven months at Parapannagrahara, being abused by the adult inmates, getting groomed into crime and cruelty towards other weaker inmates. Through all this, their mothers also got to know each other through their common struggle for trying to get bail for their sons and would often visit their children together—both at the jail and later at the OH.

Once they were brought to the OH, Sudesh and Umesh's

friendship deepened and so did their aggression. They began applying the lessons learnt in jail and bullying the younger children at the OH. Every few days, our Board received anonymous requests from the children or oral requests from the staff members, pleading with us to either grant Umesh and Sudesh bail or transfer them elsewhere as it was becoming impossible to manage them. No one was willing to lodge a formal complaint, however, as everyone was afraid that more violence would be unleashed against them if the identity of the complainant was revealed. Our Board was faced with the dilemma of whether and when to grant them bail and working on strategies to deal with the violence within the OH. Hoping that perhaps keeping them away from each other for a while might help, the JJB referred Umesh for a detailed psychological assessment to NIMHANS. Within forty-eight hours, he ran away from NIMHANS and his mother called us informing us that he had gone back home. He was brought back to the OH where he gleefully narrated his adventures to all the children and staff—who were now even more terrified of him than before.

And then a very unexpected and inexplicable thing happened. Sudesh fell in love with Meena, Umesh's mother. Sudesh had known her from the time he was at Parapannagrahara, and they had continued to meet each other every time she and his own mother came to meet their children at the OH. When he was released on bail, it was Meena's house that Sudesh went to. Soon Umesh was out on bail too. But the police would often harass Meena by taking her to the police station at odd hours and questioning her about her children's whereabouts, friends and accomplices or where they had hidden their loot. On one such occasion, Sudesh went to the police station at 1.00 am and brought

Meena home. 'No one ever did that for me, Madam,' she said quietly, when I asked her if she would like to talk to a family counsellor. 'I don't need a counsellor.' That Meena was in her mid-thirties and Sudesh was not yet 18 years old did not seem to matter to either of them.

Sudesh too came from an abusive family. His father would mercilessly beat his mother and older sister. Unable to bear this any more, Sudesh had run away from home when he was around 15 years old and started working at a bakery in faraway Odisha. Life away from home and family brought more violence, verbal and sexual abuse and abject poverty. He dreamt of becoming rich someday and taking care of his mother and sister. His dream was to start a bakery and he learned to bake bread, cake and biscuits.

But like Umesh, Sudesh was not an easy child to love— for me or for his family. When Sudesh was moved to the OH from the jail and we asked his mother why she had not filed a bail application before the Board, his mother told us that she didn't want him back home as she feared her daughter's marriage would break up because of him. Now that he was out of jail, she believed that the OH was a safe and good place for him and she was in no hurry to get him out again. This time around, instead of referring Sudesh for counselling, we referred his mother for counselling to the family counselling team at NIMHANS.

Sudesh was a really angry child who would beat and threaten every child at the OH. The violence he unleashed was particularly brutal. All the children and staff dreaded every moment that Sudesh was at the OH and waited anxiously for him to go out on bail.

Sudesh taught me that the hardest thing in the juvenile justice system is not fighting the system or lack of resources.

The hardest thing is to fight anger and unkindness within oneself. Most children, by virtue of being young and vulnerable usually invoke a natural response in me of wanting to protect and care for them. But not all children are easy to love, because some of them like Sudesh and Umesh will push all your buttons and seeing them hurt other children makes it even harder to find kindness for them within yourself. Despite all the training, it then becomes difficult to feel empathy or practice compassion. *That* is the hardest part of the work in the juvenile justice system and the danger that I think one must always guard against.

Yet, it is children like Sudesh who have forced me to stay in touch with my humanity. He reminded me that children need us to be good role models and friends rather than critics and cynics telling them that they will never amount to anything.

'I want to be a good father to Umesh and Mahesh, aunty,' Sudesh told me softly as we sat talking about what he planned to do once he got out. 'I don't want to be like my father or Meena's husband. I want to open a bakery, earn money legally and be a good family man.'

And so, on the day when his lawyer finally filed the bail application for Sudesh on behalf of his mother and our Board took up his case for discussion on bail, we did not talk about whether he was guilty of the offences that he was charged with. We took a break from the proceedings and sat in our chambers trying to understand just what kind of a child we were dealing with. We talked about who decides what kind of love is right or wrong. We talked about a young boy and his dreams of setting up a bakery and baking the most fabulous cakes in town. Of this courageous braveheart who wanted to set right the injustices meted by society to the woman he loved. We talked about how a woman does not stop wishing for love to happen merely because she becomes a mother. Sudesh taught us to change our conversation from bail, jail and crime to relationships, dreams, fears and failures—his and our own. Sudesh brought back kindness and compassion to the conversation on justice.

But not all love stories have happy endings. Sudesh was arrested for breaking into an ATM in Tumkur within a few months after being released on bail. He had turned 18 by then and was sent to Parapannagrahara jail.

My experience with Sudesh cannot allow me to forget a valuable lesson I learned—the meaning of failure. It was a reminder that I was part of the justice system that had failed to reform or rehabilitate a child. Again.

I remember reading somewhere, 'Sometimes people pretend you are a bad person so they don't feel guilty about the things they did to you.' I don't know why Sudesh always reminded me of this saying.

So are there kids out there are who are beyond reform?

I wouldn't know about that. Their stories may not all have happy endings, but I am yet to meet a child who was beyond reform, more importantly, a child who was beyond kindness.

Many of the children who come into the system are so hurt and broken by life's experiences that even they have given up on themselves. But that's exactly why we are here. To not give up on children in the justice system. To remind them and ourselves of our shared humanity. For it is in caring for these most vulnerable children of our society that we reveal our character as a society and redeem our promise to the future citizens of the world.

Sometimes the problems relating to the juvenile justice

system can feel too big, complex and overwhelming. It is easy to blame the children and even easier to blame the parents, the media, the system, and so on. Media often portrays these children as 'dangerous criminals', while some activists also tend to demonize the state and cite government apathy and poor implementation of the juvenile justice law as the biggest impediments to child protection, reform and social reintegration of children in conflict with the law. While we cannot deny that a large share of the responsibility for child protection lies with the state, blaming and demonizing does not help either.

What I Have Learned Working With Children in Conflict With the Law

> There is always one moment in childhood when the door opens and lets the future in.
>
> —Graham Greene, *The Power and the Glory*

I have found that there was a whole lot to learn from the children I worked with. These teenagers in captivity were teaching me lessons that my formal education had not helped me learn. People who must navigate the system on a daily basis ought to keep these simple but important lessons in mind:

Children in conflict with the law are just like other children. In that they crave love and a desire to belong and will do almost anything just to please an adult who promises attention, affection or appreciation in any form. This is in fact also the reason why most children are easily exploited by adult criminals and gangs.

Children in conflict with the law are not dangerous monsters or scary villains, cunning crooks, or cold remorseless criminals. Most often, they are scared children, clueless and confused teenagers, misguided and exploited youth, desperately-in-need-of-help young persons. Almost every child I've known struggled with shame, guilt, regret, remorse—but not every child knew how to convey or communicate that adequately or articulately.

Many children in conflict with the law are innocent of the offences they have been charged with. Not every child in conflict with the law is an offender. Many children are named as accomplices as they may be known to the real offender who names him as a 'friend', while many others are 'fixed' by the police; yet others get sucked into the system merely because they happen to be at or near the scene of the alleged offence.

Almost every single child in the juvenile justice system has undergone horrors that many of us can only imagine. Brutal violence, sexual abuse, emotional neglect, homelessness, abandonment by family, abject poverty—these were recurring themes in the lives of so many of the children that, after a point, I stopped counting. Multiple Adverse Childhood Experiences are a norm for every child in the juvenile justice system.

The Indian education system has little patience with those who struggle—either with family, with finances or with academics. Most of the children in conflict with the law were school dropouts or had terrible experiences with schooling. They have also never had any systematic education, and thus, in classes 8 and 10, when students sit for the State Board examinations, there is way too much to catch up with, making it virtually impossible to do so. Many children also have learning disabilities or are at the lower end of the IQ spectrum making it difficult to go through the Indian education system without any remedial support.

Almost every child in conflict with the law will have some mental health problem which has either been undetected or untreated. Many children routinely described as 'habituals', 'bad', 'undisciplined', 'dangerous', 'repeaters', etc., that I encountered in my work were suffering from serious mental health conditions and had never received any treatment for the same. This is why I believe that every single child must get a mental health assessment and appropriate treatment. Without such intervention, there is no mitigation of the risk factors that keep bringing them back into conflict with the law throughout their lives.

It is possible to teach empathy to children, and for them to heal and take responsibility for their own lives. I came to see that even as the justice system rightly demanded accountability from them for their actions, it was hard for children who had never experienced kindness or compassion themselves to understand that their behaviour could cause harm or suffering to others. Reassuringly, I also learnt that it was possible to teach them empathy and basic human decency with caregivers and adults in charge practising it themselves and setting an example through their own behaviour.

Listening, kindness, presence and genuine affection from a caring adult very often made it possible for children in conflict with the law to turn their lives around. But the child needs someone to believe in him. Someone who can see beyond his acts of negligence, violence or thoughtlessness that brought him into the system.

Some wounds are simply too deep for them to heal in weeks, months or even years. Some losses cannot be made good, in counselling or out of it. To expect that the juvenile justice system can 'reform, rehabilitate or reintegrate' children in conflict with the law while they are in Observation Homes or Special Homes is an unrealistic expectation. All we can do as mental health professionals or child protection professionals is to hold children and their families through the turbulent times and hope that the storms will pass, that time and support will help us all heal from the harm we have suffered—as victims, as offenders and as a community, and that we will all emerge stronger and wiser for having gone through these turbulent experiences in our lives.

Parents, counsellors, lawyers and judges are all human too. Though each tries their hand at playing God, in the end, we are all fallible, flawed human beings struggling to make our part of the world a slightly better place. This means we have to hold each other up, we must connect and be supportive towards each other as this is a tough job and place to work— one that demands every last one of our reserves, both mental and physical.

Burn-out and fatigue are real and we can continue our work in this area only if we have found a way to keep ourselves going. This is a challenge in itself.

What keeps me going? I don't find it easy. It certainly isn't fulfilling on most occasions especially given that one is up against systematic oppression. But it has its moments. It is those moments I live for.

But the system shouldn't be premised merely on the guarantee that skilled professionals will keep committing themselves to this work for little more than such 'moments', however profound.

The promise of the Juvenile Justice Act is the social reintegration of vulnerable children who have fallen out of the safety net of the family and community. It's driven by the solemn hope that the legal system can restore their dignity and give these children a second chance at life where the social system has failed to do so. For this promise to be kept, counsellors need systemic support from the state and civil society in the form of better administrative and infrastructural support, competitive remuneration for professional services rendered, career growth opportunities, professionally trained support teams, and acknowledgement and appreciation of the invaluable contribution made by them to the lives of thousands of children.

No one can do this work alone. For counsellors to be more than just mental health professionals, and actually serve as advocates and champions of the rights of the children in the justice system, we must learn to look at them as frontline warriors in the battle for justice and well-being of these children. These gentle warriors of health, hope and healing need the community to mentor, support and nurture them for the 'best interest' of these neglected children enshrined in the law to actually mean something.

'MAIN BHI INSAAN HOON'
(*I Too Am Human*)

Puneeta Roy

Being deeply loved by someone gives you strength, while loving someone deeply gives you courage.

—Lao Tzu, Chinese philosopher

Each one of us needs love. We all crave for understanding, for dignity and respect. But how many are fortunate to receive these basic human rights that should be freely accessible to all?

Vaibhav is a young offender who is a part of our weekly workshop group at the Place of Safety & Special Home for Boys, Majnu ka Tila. He was 16 years old when an intimate relationship resulted in him being infected with HIV. A year and a half later, he is an emotional mess.

Too ashamed to share this dark truth with his family, he has spent the past nine months between Tihar Jail and the Observation Home at Majnu ka Tila, implicated on what he calls 'false charges'. The magistrate is ready to release him, but at the moment, he would rather cloak his shame within the confines of the Observation Home than face his family.

Vaibhav has refused to see his family these past few months, but the fragility and trauma of this boy in desperate need for support and understanding is obvious even to a casual visitor. Petrified of exposing his family to the virus, he had to be calmed by explaining the possible forms of transmission and the precautionary measures that can keep his family members safe from getting infected.

It is clear, however, that we need an extensive support system to educate and counsel numerous 'at-risk' youth so that their sexual and mental health is not endangered.

A property dispute within the family after the sudden death of his father; an elder brother who sought to reclaim the rights of his mother and, in a violent altercation, stabbed his own cousin brother; and the resultant hardships of a hand-to-mouth existence of this tiny ostracized family—little wonder that young Adil had no guide, no role model to stop him as he slipped into the world of drugs and crime, small deviations expanding into larger ones as his needs and ambitions went up. Barely 18 years now, Adil today is the father of an infant daughter, whom he absolutely adores and is determined to clean up his act for.

Does he have the required skillset to be able to eke out a living for his small family? Will society give him a chance to make a new beginning?

Overcrowded classrooms, school curricula that doesn't engage the boys, the swag of the cool, macho gang that lures them to bunk class and gravitate towards the neighbourhood park for a casual smoke—the slip is so gradual that before he even realizes it, the young boy has been lured into the world of drugs, gambling and petty crime. A slide that gets dangerous when he is inducted into 'gangs' of adult criminals who use these boys as runners initially and then train them to become more useful members. A treacherous slope from which few can return. The enemies of the rival gang become *their* enemies and 'shoot or be shot' situations become only too frequent. Very Bollywood-esque! Indeed, the 'Dons' of Bollywood, and its often glamorous portrayal of the underworld, continue to be their inspiration.

My first meeting with children in conflict with law is at the Adharshila Observation Home for Boys, Sewa Kutir, Kingsway Camp, Delhi, in the year 2008, after a chance encounter with Justice Madan B. Lokur, former judge, Supreme Court of India. Known for his keen interest in juvenile justice, he asks in his quiet, gentle manner if I am willing to work with a section of youth who are 'invisible' to society, stigmatized and condemned for life. He speaks of Children in Conflict with Law, i.e. CICL.

I am intrigued. I have no special skillset to work in Observation Homes except a passion and belief that every young person deserves a chance in life, and the wish, if within my means, to provide such an opportunity.

As I arrive at the Adharshila Observation Home and walk through the corridors into the rooms, I look at faces that are no different from the hundreds of young adults I have worked with these past few years, in private and government schools across Delhi. Some are angry, some turn away, many stare back, curious, wondering what an outsider like me is doing there. A few are clearly petrified as they anticipate what awaits them in the Home.

I speak with them, hear their stories and I know I cannot walk away.

Navigating the World of Children in Conflict With the Law

My humanity is bound up in yours, for we can only be human together.

—Desmond Tutu,
South African bishop and theologian

Thereon begins a fascinating journey of bringing the world of theatre and expressive arts into the lives of these young offenders. Most of them have been so starved of emotional nourishment and nurture that their sense of Self is practically non-existent. A frozen cache of dreams veering towards the 'impossible' and a complete absence of agency to carve out a respectable life for themselves has made them vulnerable to exploitation and abuse.

What better tool than the arts to ignite a sense of 'Who I Am?', to help discover themselves through the rich tapestry of creative expression that it offers?

Theatre, music, dance, puppetry, creative writing, drawing and painting are some of the tools we offer.

A fundamental theme of our theatre workshops is exploring their dreams and aspirations, resulting in several performances at the Home. 'Main Bhi Insaan Hoon' is a stirring enactment that the boys put up for their parents as well as the visiting magistrates and officials, the outcome of a month-long workshop that explores their humanity and resonates deeply with the boys.

A daily morning workshop at the *kharja* (the waiting room outside the Juvenile Justice Board) as the boys wait for their bail hearing, turns into a three-year intervention at Sahyog, the de-addiction centre run by the Society for

Promotion of Youth and Masses (SPYM), where these workshops are held regularly over a five-day week.

Robbery, murder, rape, extortion seem to be common offences the boys have been charged with. Most feel they have been falsely implicated, that the system is working against them, and that they are not responsible for the crimes they are being incarcerated for. They believe they had no option, that circumstances forced them into doing what they did. Feeling rejected by society, many of them are filled with anger and vengeance.

'This time I will ensure that there will be no half murder charge; it will be the real kill!'

'Once I am out I will commit a really big robbery, so that if I am caught, it would at least have been worth it!'

The rebelliousness of adolescence coupled with the headiness of being a 'gang member' can be an intoxicating cocktail.

However, one size doesn't fit all. At the Adharshila Home I introduce a weekly environment awareness programme and ask how many would like to plant trees and take care of them. Five hands go up; Rahul in fact is specific. He asks me to bring a tulsi plant to put in the mandir in his dorm.

I push open the crack and reach out to him.

'Mandir? Do you believe in God then?'

'Yes of course, I believe in God, Didi! Don't you?'

'Hmm…I do. Tell me, where does your God reside?'

'In the mandir that is within my heart!'

'And when you picked up a knife to kill, where did your God go?'

'Didi, the doors of my temple were open long before and my God left me. I am waiting for him to return!'

I look back into Rahul's earnest eyes with a lump in my throat. What childlike innocence despite the ruthless thrusts that hand can make! My challenge is to make these young people aware of the choices they have in every situation, choices that empower rather than debilitate them.

On my next visit, the tulsi is tucked firmly under my arm. Rahul's eyes shine in gratitude as he receives it and Amarjeet, his best friend, asks him, 'Now do you believe your God is back!'

This one statement will resonate with me for a long time. As I turn away to leave the Home, both Rahul and Amarjeet come up to me and tell me that their bail might come through in the next couple of days. How will they meet me again if they are released?

'Don't you have to come back here once a week for counselling even when you get bail?'

They are not sure, but Amarjeet promises to leave a drawing for me if he is released before the next class.

I walk away with moist eyes at this gesture of generosity and affection. So quick to give love, so easy to express it! I find myself almost hoping that these two are not released so soon; they can be excellent peer educators within my programme at the Home. But the next time I come to the Observation Home, an evocative drawing of a village hut under the arc of a tree has been left behind for me.

Creating a Safe Environment: The Workshop Spaces

Love has nothing to do with what you are expecting to get. Only with what you are expecting to give—which is everything!

—Katherine Hepburn, American actor

We are the outsiders here, offering a theatre-based expressive arts programme that does not enhance their legal aid, but which we hope will definitely help them with their overall confidence and sense of well-being. Slowly, the boys begin to step out of their comfort zone to explore new spaces, connecting to each other in new ways, as they become sensitive to the vibes we emit and receive.

Predominant are their memories of hurt and betrayal. When asked to share one emotion they have felt strongly, most talk about the anger that drives them, the hatred that burns deep within. A few recall the happiness they have felt with a loved one. It's clear we need to explore their emotional energies much deeper and teach them how to be alert to understand and release these energies, without being destructive.

This is uncharted territory and we will have to draw our own road map. How best can we get them to respond? Is there an ideal time frame? An ideal format? It takes trial and more trial, adapting to the Home and the availability of the boys, who may have their court hearing come up on that day, or an overdue doctor's visit, or may simply not be in the mood to engage with us through a workshop.

Starting with small groups of ten each, weekly visits spread over three months to become intense ten-day sessions, stretching at times into month-long summer workshops held on alternate days. Various permutations and combinations yield due results, as the boys open up to more constructive interactions with the world outside.

Performances for the staff and other inmates are held, and we organize cricket matches with other NGOs like Salaam Baalak Trust, as well as corporates engaging with them as part of their corporate social responsibility. It is exhilarating to see their growth as they open up to our workshops, even as they struggle with adapting to a structure, the lack of a support system and a deep despair about how long the judicial system takes to respond to their cases.

Most of the boys languish in the Homes waiting for their court hearing, and when they do get called before the Board, it is only to be given a date for the next hearing! This naturally builds up frustration and helplessness within the boys and a lack of faith in a system that de-humanizes them. Obviously, this impacts our work in the Home, and we face a backlash just when we seem to be making crucial headway with the boys. Almost abruptly, they block us out and withdraw their trust, reacting to a betrayal that has happened within the Home or in the courts. Sometimes, they are even instigated by their 'gangs' in the Home to take revenge or to teach another boy or group a 'lesson', and they must face the same brutality within the Home that they have had to deal with outside.

Trust. We rediscover the value of this word, this emotion. How difficult it must be to trust another human, when all your life you have faced only betrayal!

Why would these young people trust us? To them, we are complete strangers who have picked them randomly for 'workshops'.

What do we actually want to know from them? How will we use this information?

I see these questions fleeting through their minds as we continue doggedly to work with various batches at the Observation Home and the de-addiction centre. As we grapple with the complexity of the entire eco-system within which juvenile crime exists, I wonder if we have any clear answers to those questions.

Testing Our Methods

> Our human compassion binds us the one to the other—not in pity or patronizingly but as human beings who have learnt how to turn our common suffering into hope for the future.
>
> —Nelson Mandela

As we try to join the dots for ourselves, a prompt by Justice Lokur to document our work and offer empirical evidence about the efficacy of art-based therapy in the Indian context leads us to our most challenging project in this field. The result is our 2022 research study titled *Building Emotional Intelligence and Self Esteem with Children in Conflict with Law using Expressive Arts and Psychodrama Therapy*.

We choose a new home, the Place of Safety & Special Home for Boys at Majnu ka Tila, Delhi, because we need to work with a consistent group for a period of one year. The inmates here are older than those we have worked with at Sewa Kutir and Sahyog and have a reputation of being more difficult and challenging.

From a total of approximately sixty boys, a group of twenty-five young adults are picked through random chits, and they constitute our Intervention/Experiment Group. The boys are from 18 to 21 years of age and have been charged with or found guilty of various heinous crimes ranging from murder, rape, sodomy to kidnapping and burglary, among others. They are mirrored by another twenty-five young persons who form our Control Group.

All fifty boys go through a rigorous series of pre-test sessions on emotional intelligence and self-esteem, conducted by our team of trained psychologists and research assistants, distinct from the workshop facilitation team. Starting from June 2018 all the way to May 2019, the Intervention Group is exposed to fifty sessions of expressive arts and ten sessions of psychodrama therapy. These are interspersed with mid-session tests on emotional intelligence with both groups, as well as a final wrap of post-session tests at the end.

It is the first time we are working with a consistent group of CICL for such a prolonged period of time. In the initial few months, we hold sessions twice a week, and to be honest, they take a toll on us facilitators.

Between planning, conducting and reviewing the sessions, there is little time or energy left for anything else. It is not as if the boys have been welcoming us with open arms either. Nor have we made it easy for them by starting our sessions at 9:30 am in the morning. For those of them used to living by their own clock, this is a painful start to the day. Each group has its own hierarchies, the 'bhais' who flaunt their obvious clout with swag. It kills them to be treated as equals within our workshop structure, especially as we go about breaking the ice among groups, get them to play games, draw, paint, act and dance, whilst constantly asking them to share their emotions—quite a hefty ask, we realize later! These young adults have taken on the law and expect due respect to be given to that.

Different boys snap at different times. Most feel vulnerable being 'in the spotlight', resist sharing emotions or stories, refuse to dance or enact any theatre exercises as it opens them up to ridicule once they return to their common dorms in the Home after the workshop.

Jai is the volatile cocktail in our group. Charming, sharp, needing constant attention and nurture, he has one of the

most fragile egos in the room that shouts its warning—
'Handle with Care'! Talented, with clear artistic inclinations,
Jai has been quite a Dada within the Home and desperately
wants us to recognize that.

Initially, it is quite a clash of wills between us. An art
activity aimed at creating emotional awareness is responded
to by drawing cartoons from a reference book he is carrying
into the class. The defiance turns into insolence and quickly
into hostility as we try to create a level playing field for all,
something he has tried to painstakingly demolish within the
Home. The disrespect reaches a point where we tell him to
sit out a couple of sessions.

A subdued Jai returns to our sessions after we reach out
to him on a one-to-one level and initiate a conversation of
mutual respect. He begins to understand that our efforts to
make them emotionally aware is not to mock or humiliate
them, but to enable them to recognize their own emotions
and manage them better. Thereby leading to more empowered
choices.

Now he misses the sessions when they don't happen and
is open and forthright with us about his feelings.

Jai's response to the Mask Making Activity. Left: Outer Mask: Happy, sunny,
radiant. Right: Inner Mask: Angry, aggressive, violent.

It takes time and patience but we manage to gently weave a net of dignity and respect that criss-crosses across groups and connects each boy to us, creating bonds of warmth and acceptance that slowly dissolve their mistrust.

We explain the intent of our project to them right from the outset. But have to repeat this at practically every session. We are here to collect data on the efficacy of art and theatre in building emotional intelligence among young offenders, which we intend to present to the Ministry of Women & Child Development, urging them to start expressive arts therapy in every Children's Home in the country.

Twenty-five pairs of eyes watch every move, register every nuance, as we navigate through an environment that is not exactly hostile, but unreceptive in the beginning. Each session has been meticulously planned, our intent spelt out and the graph of the workshop mapped, with even a Plan B worked out. Most times we manage to complete the task we have set for the session. The boys are slowly opening up but some of the more 'macho' ones still hide behind a wall of defences, and when at their most vulnerable, the carefully maintained facade of civility cracks.

Samarth has a mind of his own. He came to the workshops slightly aloof and disinterested but gradually found a space for himself. There are times when he enjoys painting. It feels like he will forget his worries and submerge himself completely in the experience. Working with his hands and cherishing the labour in his fields which he misses, he finds his calling in clay modelling. Peaceful, quiet and creative, he shares how much he misses the mud.

He often reminisces about his life in the village and as he gets comfortable with us, he begins to immerse himself fully in the exercises. But there is never one story with Samarth. His participation in the workshops has been sporadic and volatile.

The first cracks begin to appear on a day we are painting CDs. As we do generally, we interact with each participant to ask a few questions about the process. Upon approaching him, quite out of nowhere, he breaks his CD into pieces. Irate and unflinching, nothing makes any sense to him and the anger is palpable in his clenched fists as he leaves the room.

Next week he returns with the same fresh smile that we are used to. When we talk about the task for the day, he refuses to do it. Given our interaction with him the week before, we ask him to take up a corner and be around even if he is not willing to participate. One of us sits with him and gives him a mandala to paint. He is happy to work on his own, without having to interact with the others. '*Mujhe bas ap aise hi kagaz aur rang de diya karo, main yahin kone mein baith jaunga, bakiyon ke saath kaam nahin karunga.*' (Just give me paper and colours in each class, I will sit in a corner and work alone.)

As he settles down I ask about his outburst last week. He does not mince his words. He shares that he was unhappy about 'that' woman's dressing sense, referring to an intern at the Home who has been visiting the workshop space for a few weeks. The conversation deepens. We talk about gender, choices and the responses of men.

Samarth's participation in the workshops becomes more erratic. He arrives at the workshops only when he feels like participating. When we bump into him accidentally at the Home, he politely smiles and laughs with us, tells us he won't come, only to turn up the following week and sit quietly in the corner. Slowly, it dawns on us that there are clear symptoms of bi-polarity in Samarth that need to be addressed. The workshop space is not enough to take care of his mental and psychological needs. Assisted with a proper psychiatric programme, the impact of our expressive arts workshops would increase manifold. We express our concerns to the counsellor at the Home, making a mental note that we need to add a counsellor and psychologist to the services that we offer.

A year later, our relationship with Samarth is as vibrant and chirpy as ever. He meets us, greets us, shakes hands and keeps reminding us that he would need photographs of his artworks before being released. He has resumed coming to the workshops, is not hostile or disruptive, and it is amazing to see him enjoying painting and creative writing in the workshop.

Consistency begins to pay. Meeting us week upon week, month after month, surprised that we are not discouraged by their hostility or rude behaviour but continue with love and enthusiasm, slowly starts winning the boys over. Many start participating and enjoy the activities, even sharing their emotions within smaller groups. We all start looking forward to the workshop sessions.

Over the months our group has been getting smaller as a few boys are released, or are out on bail. When the bone ossification test for age determination shows them to be older than 18 years, they are sent to Tihar Jail. It is painful for us when this happens as by now we have formed personal relationships with each of them. As our target of completing fifty sessions gets closer, our visits to the Home are now spaced out to once a week, much to the consternation of the group, who would now like to see us five days in a week.

27/09/2018

मेरे में क्लास में आने के बाद बहुत बदलाव आया है।

मैं चाहता हूँ, की मैं वैसे ही अच्छा बनने की कोशिश करूँ जैसे मैं क्लास में बनता हूँ।

मैं आगे भी छूटने के बाद अच्छी संगत में रहना चाहता हूँ, जैसे यहाँ होता हूँ।

मुझे drawing करना नहीं आता था, पर अब आने लगा है। पहले मुझे यह लगता था कि ये कैसे होगा, पर अब मेरे अंदर बनाने की जागरूकता है।

Rijul sir, Puneeta Ma'am और Bhanu Ma'am के साथ अलग-अलग कला सीखने को मिली। मैं सबको तहे दिल से धन्यवाद दूँगा।

Samarth's reflections in his private journal, dated 27/09/2018.

Each boy is given an individual Art Kit consisting of a diary, a box of crayons, a box of colour pencils, a ruler, pencil and eraser. Almost 50 percent of the boys cannot read or write, despite going to school in their initial years. We transcribe their thoughts as they share them with us.

Samarth shares the change that has come over him after attending our 'class'. He hopes to sustain this positive change even outside and keep good company when he leaves this home. Earlier, he could not draw but now has begun to make the effort. He is grateful to the facilitators for the different skills he has learnt from each one of them.

Ranging from curiosity to downright hostility, the boys go through a range of emotions that reflect in the build-up of trust and friendship with us.

The Ganesh we meet initially is quiet, eyes mostly downcast, not willing to engage much and talking only when spoken to. We soon learn that he is intelligent, articulate and extremely frustrated at being locked away on a kidnapping charge, an anger that finds an outlet through our mask masking activity, in which his Outer Self is smiling but his Inner Self is outraged, with bloodied eyes and a grimacing mouth.

Ganesh blossoms visibly with the introduction of drawing and painting. Never having held a crayon before, he has grown a lot more confident, takes risks and is willing to experiment with his art work. As he moves gradually from small sketches to larger canvasses, we are overjoyed to see the outpouring of colour and form. The sense of satisfaction is visible on his face as he explains—'*Colour dekhte hi mere haath chalne lagte hain.*'

Today it's a much happier Ganesh who has been reading a lot of Munshi Premchand's stories, and is no longer scared of being different, or putting himself out there. He regrets the act that got him into the Home and we are sure that given the right mentoring, Ganesh can definitely make something constructive out of his life.

Mihir has been the ever smiling, the 'always wanting to please' member of our group. His pleasant countenance belies the fact that he is here on a rape charge, which he confesses happened under the influence of drugs. In our initial interactions, he is low on confidence, afraid of making mistakes and being judged. Each time after an activity is explained, he calls one of the facilitators and asks for a

Clear skies, a bright sunny day and a tranquil ocean. Ganesh is happy on the deck of the steamer as the lighthouse guides him to the land—a positive affirmation of his current state of mind.

Expressing his newly discovered love for the stories of Munshi Premchand, as a source of inner strength.

separate explanation just so that he can reassure himself that he has understood. '*Karna kya hai?*' he would ask repeatedly.

As the year progresses, Mihir's confidence has grown visibly. Apart from enjoying drawing, he is one of the few who can read and write, and has articulated his emotions well in his journal. Now he has slowly started helping others by writing for them in their journals.

Today Mihir is the first to participate in any activity and he waits for every Wednesday morning because we remind him of the importance of values like empathy and compassion.

He is reflective when asked about his plans once released—'*Pata nahin mai kya karunga. Par workshop mei aap jaise humse baat karte hain, mujhe bahut achha lagta hai. Bahar jaakar mai kuch aisi cheez karoonga jisse samaj mujhe vaise hi izzat de!*' (I am not sure what I'll do once I'm released. But I love the respect accorded to me in the workshop. I will make ensure that whatever I do once out will earn me the same respect in society.)

A few boys show promise initially but slowly become a bunch of diminishing returns. Most of these are school dropouts and find it difficult to sustain focus for too long. They find it stressful to keep up with the class, even though we are constantly looking out for the back benchers. We hope that the love and respect we accord them enables some of the healing process to begin.

Halfway through the project we have a flash of insight!

More than merely requesting for participation from the boys, we need to impart a sense of ownership, of pride in belonging to a project that respects them and is genuinely working towards their self-empowerment.

An 'Open Day' is the answer. We open the gates of the

Mihir's response to the House-Tree-Person Assessment test, that measures a person's psychological and emotional functioning.

Reflecting on the positive aspect of ourselves as that which gives us courage, and the negative as that aspect that distances us from others.

Place of Safety & Special Home for Boys at Majnu ka Tila, to welcome well-wishers and responsible citizens to view the project work done by the boys over the past few months. The workshops have become more flexible as we share our vision with the boys and respond to their suggestions as well.

The excitement is palpable as the date of the Open Day approaches and we race to gather their stories, their paintings, drawings, collages, their puppets and mud sculptures and display them in the most creative fashion possible.

Each boy is in charge of explaining a different exhibit to the visitors. When a visiting magistrate, or a family member walks up to anyone of our participants, asking them about the intent of a particular exercise, the responses of the boys, the pride on their faces and in their voices is palpable. To engage with a 'respectable' member of the community and receive appreciation for their work is a huge fillip to their sense of self-worth and self-esteem.

It is easier now to negotiate with our young friends through activities that continue to challenge them. We continually push the bar as the pace becomes swifter to take them along with us. Another Open Day gives an additional boost of confidence, and by March, we begin the process of winding down as the end of the project looms ahead.

'Will you leave us now and go?'

'Are there going to be no more workshops?'

'Will we not meet you after this?'

Initially a bit plaintive, the questions get angry and resentful as the end of the project nears: 'Why did you come if you were going to leave?'

It is not easy for us either to say our goodbyes to our group. Stepping in as strangers among an unknown group, we are now one family. We have come to understand the

The workshops have become their own now!

A display of their work at the Open Day when they explain their work to magistrates, the Superintendent of the Home and outside visitors.

joys and sorrows of each boy, the legal status of their case, of whether they feel hopeful of their future or are stuck in a quagmire of cynicism and crime.

Wrap up with this Intervention Group we must but even as we complete our post-session tests, we offer them a shorter module based on voluntary participation, giving some the option to move out.

Two-thirds of the group want to continue. We open it up to members of the Control Group who have been asking when they can participate in the activities, and a month later, Intervention 2 begins. This is a much easier ride because we are applying the lessons of openness and flexibility we learned in our previous intervention.

Learning Outcomes: Setting Further Goals

> Keep your face always toward the sunshine, and shadows will fall behind you.
>
> —Walt Whitman,
> American poet and humanist

We understand that our work at the Place of Safety and Special Home for Boys will be incomplete if we do not offer our programme to the maximum number of young offenders, so that the general levels of anger and aggression within the Home can come down. As we collate the findings of our research, we continue to work with different batches, shifting to an online model to maintain our connection with the boys all through the Covid pandemic.

The Covid pandemic hit the boys badly. Following the lockdown protocols across the country, all family visits are halted, and the boys can speak to their loved ones once a

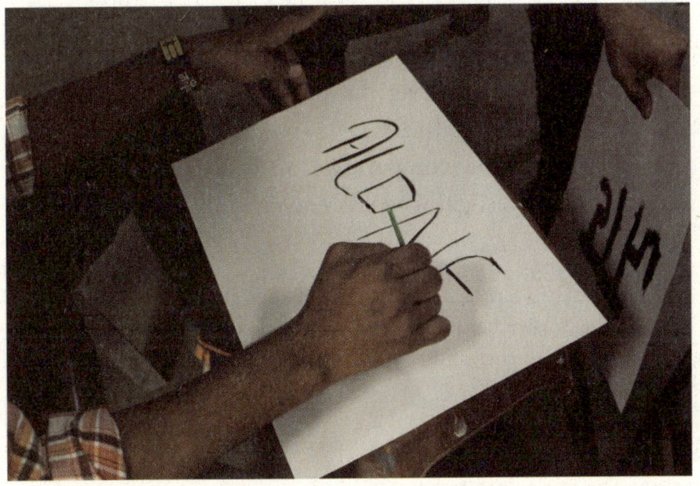

Their isolation and loneliness is compounded by the pandemic.

week at most. Feelings of isolation and anxiety run high as family becomes a big cause of worry and anxiety for almost everyone.

It becomes necessary to reduce numbers in the Observation Home. Several boys are sent home on parole, including boys like Arun and Sameer who have been refused bail on several occasions and are stepping out into the world after almost five years. With what trepidation would they have re-entered their neighbourhood, absorbing the changed landscape and altered dynamics within and outside their own homes. They try to re-integrate back into the earlier structure as they pick up the threads with their families. Sameer starts helping his father with his cooler-repair business, enjoying the feeling of being a 'free man' though ostensibly on parole, relishing his mother's hot parathas and loving care.

Just as suddenly, as the pandemic comes under control, a notice is sent out to all the boys asking them to return by a particular date. Reluctantly, they come back, hoping this would count as 'good behaviour' and will help them get bail soon. The courts, however, have their own procedures, and the waiting game continues.

Meanwhile, the comparative analysis prepared by our co-principal investigator yields encouraging results:

No.	Pre-Tests (0 months)	Post-Tests (12 months)
1.	Aggressive behaviour with other inmates and staff	Reduced aggression and improved sense of calm
2.	Hopelessness and gloominess	Increased state of happiness
3.	Stubborn and difficult behaviour	Less stubborn, more cooperative and more open to giving way to others
4.	Signs of low self-worth and self-confidence	Improved self-esteem and confidence through positive reinforcement
5.	No value seen in the therapeutic process and sense of 'forced' participation in the process	Improved sense of ownership and recognition of progress made through the artistic process
6.	Complete mistrust and suspicion of the motives of the project team	Complete trust in the project team and reliance on their presence
7.	Limited regret for crime committed and low motivation to choose the right path	Looking at walking on the right path, improving their own lives and becoming respectable citizens

No.	Pre-Tests (0 months)	Post-Tests (12 months)
8.	No respect for other people and their boundaries	Improved respect for other people—peers and staff, facilitators—and their boundaries
9.	Only concerned with their own point of view and low tolerance for others' perspectives	Increased ability to put themselves in other people's shoes and looking at their perspectives
10.	Not able to wait for others	Improved patience and ability to move at other people's pace
11.	Not in touch with their own emotions	Improved awareness of their own emotions and recognizing the importance of speaking about emotions

Based on the cumulative scores and assessment through various tools, we find that:

- Self-esteem has shown significant improvement in the group.
- A positive change can be seen in the levels of intrapersonal awareness.
- Participants feel happier and calmer and tend to stay more stable and focused.
- There's an improvement in clarity of thought, leading to more coherence and logical thinking.
- More control over anger and an improved ability to take their time to think before reacting.

Most of these changes have been corroborated by the staff and caregivers at the Home. This spurs us to continue our work.

In the meantime Ganesh and Mihir have both been released on bail. Ganesh is finally at peace with his widowed mother and has started to help ease her financial burden. At the moment he is working in a delivery agency and has cut all ties with his former friends. Mihir too has adjusted well back into his family. Initially trying his hand at different occupations, from a home furniture shop to the repair of air conditioner stabilizers, he has settled in a hardware store close to his home, as his family makes plans for his wedding.

Since our initial research programme in 2018, we have worked with five more batches. As our understanding of the boys deepens, we are bolder in our approach and introduce newer themes such as Power & Vulnerability, Boundaries & Safe Spaces, Toxic Masculinity, Gender Inequality, pushing them to reflect on relationships that define them.

'Softer' qualities of kindness, empathy and compassion are also discussed as we speak to them about the importance of 'giving' what they want to receive, especially love, warmth and respect.

Many boys feel their only safe space is within their own homes. We have started conversations now as to how they can create a safe space for themselves within the Observation Home itself, where they can trust themselves and others and not live in fear.

But lines have been blurring rapidly between what is socially acceptable and what is not, between the lawmakers and the lawbreakers. The 'Jaat' boys we meet from Haryana last year as part of Batch 3 have been sucked into rival gangs

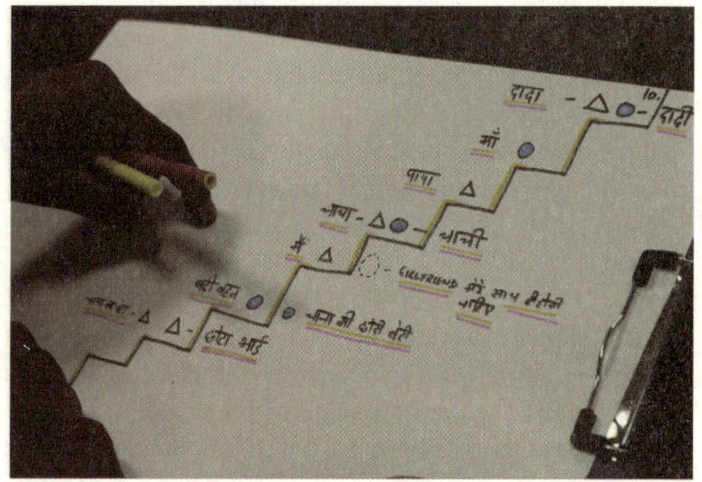

Exploring Toxic Masculinity and Gender Roles in the family.

Most boys miss their mother the most, and regret causing her grief and pain.

and the enmity extends into the Observation Home too. When gangster Jitender Maan alias Gogi is shot dead in the Rohini courtroom by members of the Tillu Tajpuria gang, a fight breaks out in the Home at Majnu ka Tila, as his young supporters grieve and want to avenge his death, suspecting that the rival group is celebrating. It is heart-wrenching to see these strong young boys with so much talent and opportunity being misled by ruthless murderers and extortionists, serving 'jail time' to satisfy their gang leader's personal greed and gain.

But despite disruptions, often violent ones like that mentioned above, after four years at the Place of Safety at Majnu ka Tila, the transformation within each boy is visible. They arrive at the workshop freshly bathed, donning a smart pair of clothes and shoes, looking forward to spending a productive two hours with us.

Their manner of speaking has changed, they are more polite and respectful with us and towards each other—something they say that they have learned from us. Many accept their crime and want a future away from violence and hate. But few have completed their schooling, and the road ahead isn't likely to be easy.

Looking Within

To love and be loved is to feel the sun from both sides.

—David Viscott, American psychiatrist

'The power of Love!' One tiny phrase sums up the huge learning I have received after inviting these young adults into my life. Many of them experienced little or no love in their

Kunal shares his story through the 6PSM Model.

He accepts the wrong step that brought him here. He is intelligent and articulate, has completed Class 10 and looks forward to studying further.

An artwork by one of the boys. The heart that he has drawn has four parts, for his mother, father, sister and brother.

lives and hence have negated themselves almost completely. No guidance, no appreciation, none of the 'positive strokes' that we all hunger for. It's little wonder that they seek refuge in a miasma of alcohol, drugs and false bravado.

At times I receive a telephone call out of the blue. The caller on the other end identifies himself as a young man I have worked with years ago, in the Sewa Kutir complex. Today, he has cleaned up his drug habit, has a respectable job and has kept my number safe in a scrap of paper, so that he can call one day and let me know how well he is doing. It has been a particularly emotionally draining day and his call is just the tonic I need to energize me.

On another occasion, I walk into the Majnu ka Tila home for the workshop one morning and a smart young police constable comes up to me with a big smile and asks me if I recognize him.

'Anubhav!'

One sharp look transports me back in time when Anubhav was at the Sahyog De-addiction Center and was finding it difficult to kick his drug habit.

Here he is, a strapping young man, looking back at me with clear eyes, so proud to share his recent induction into the police force. Another shot in the arm to renew my faith and hope.

How can we turn away from these young people, so lost and so misled? If one of our own children wanders across to the 'dark side', do we not give them a second chance? Do we stop believing in them altogether? Why then do we view these children through a different lens? What will it take for us to consider them as human as us?

Looking Forward

> We are very, very small, but we are profoundly capable of very, very big things.
>
> —Stephen Hawking,
> English physicist and cosmologist

A couple of years into this work we realize the import of imparting skill training, so that the older boys have a possible source of income when they are released.

In the initial years of our intervention at the Adharshila Observation Home, Sewa Kutir, The Kirloskar Brothers step in to offer electrical and pump mechanic training—three batches of ten boys complete three months of training each. Many stay the course and are placed in internships across the city. Unfortunately, only one boy manages to complete the internship period of a year. That is when I realize the urgent need of a mentoring system, to hand-hold the boys for at least two years after their release, to make the transition into re-integration smoother.

This is at the core of the helplessness I echo—the urgency for the justice delivery system to be sensitive and proactive in bringing about the rehabilitation and rebuilding of young lives, and not focus on retribution.

It is a challenge that we, as a society, have to find an answer to. Return to school programmes, vocational training and placement in jobs could enable these young men and women re-integrate back into mainstream society, empowering the 'have-nots' into becoming the best versions of themselves. Work has to be done with their families and at the community level too.

Our hunt continues for funds and partners, to expand the canvas of our work and deepen our intervention, to offer expertise in terms of legal aid, mental health services as well as vocational skill training. I would urge everyone to take time out of their busy lives and volunteer to share a skillset with any one of these young boys. Enter their world to understand what 'boundaries' are all about—physical, mental and emotional. They talk, vulnerable and confused, about how far they are from a solution to the problems they face in life. Help them reflect on their journey ahead, as they draw a bridge linking the past to their goals and objectives that passes through where they currently find themselves.

There is the hero and the predator in each one of us—the positive and negative aspects of ourselves. Whom do we give power to, who controls our lives, and in which situations, is what defines us.

Let us change the prevailing narrative of aggression to one of peace and compassion, and commit to refine models of intervention and empowerment that can be scaled up and replicated with children in conflict with the law across the country.

ACKNOWLEDGEMENTS

This book has been in the making for many years—ever since I first began my journey into the world of children. They have taught me everything I know today. These children have opened up their lives to me and taught me not to judge them for their actions, but instead to appreciate the circumstances that led them to be where they are. They have also made me believe that every child deserves a chance.

I also owe my own learning to my colleagues who have struggled with me, activists and practitioners in India and across countries—Ann Skelton, Bernard Boeton, Benoit Van Keirsbilck, Cedric Foussard, Nevena Vuckovic Sahovic, Ton Liefaard, and all those others who have included me in their discussions, meetings and conferences.

I am grateful to all those persons who have shared their thoughts and experiences included in this book.

I thank Puneeta Roy and Kalpana Purushothaman for joining me in writing this book.

Although I always thought of writing a book like this, it would have remained just that—a thought—had it not been for Renuka Chatterjee who convinced me to take the plunge.

I thank Nazeef Mollah for editing the book and putting up with my many changes. I hope through the process of editing of this book he too has got converted to the need for 'juvenile justice'!

And finally, I must acknowledge my family—Kishore Thukral, my spouse and lifelong friend; my children, Shiuli (Bonu), and Atish (Zebu), whose story I have shared in the book; my parents who never stopped believing in me and my sister, Meenakshi. To them all I owe the time and attention that I could not give, because the children as in the book were demanding it.

THIS LAND IS MINE, I AM NOT OF THIS LAND
CAA–NRC and the Manufacture of Statelessness

Edited by Harsh Mander and Navsharan Singh

The Citizenship Amendment Act (CAA), passed by the Parliament of India in December 2019, promises citizenship to migrants of the 'Hindu, Sikh, Buddhist, Jain, Parsi or Christian community from Afghanistan, Bangladesh or Pakistan'. By excluding Muslims from the list and not extending the promise to refugees from any of India's non-Muslim-majority neighbours, the CAA makes religion the basis of citizenship for the first time in the history of the Republic. Many fear that this Act, coupled with a countrywide National Register of Citizens (NRC), will eventually be used to disenfranchise India's Muslims, or to trap them in a permanent state of fear and insecurity, which has been the fate of millions of Bengali-origin Muslims of Assam.

This Land Is Mine, I Am Not of This Land brings together a comprehensive selection of essays that deal with the theoretical, political and subjective aspects of this issue. The first section traces the evolution of citizenship in India. The following section deals with the peculiar case of Assam. Covered here are the bureaucratic travesties unleashed in the name of protecting the state from 'external aggression' as well as their sobering human cost. The concluding sections expose the superfluousness of the National Population Register (NPR), and pose serious questions on the constitutionality of the CAA.

The book argues that with a key value like citizenship in question, it is not just the destinies of India's citizens but the very democratic foundation of the Republic that is at stake.